OXFORD
Literacy
Skills

2

Geoff Barton
Richard Broomhead
Fiona Edwards
Julie Macey

OXFORD
UNIVERSITY PRESS

Great Clarendon Street, Oxford OX2 6DP

Oxford University Press is a department of the University of Oxford.
It furthers the University's objective of excellence in research, scholarship,
and education by publishing worldwide in

Oxford New York

Athens Auckland Bangkok Bogotá Buenos Aires Calcutta
Cape Town Chennai Dar es Salaam Delhi Florence Hong Kong Istanbul
Karachi Kuala Lumpur Madrid Melbourne Mexico City Mumbai
Nairobi Paris São Paulo Shanghai Singapore Taipei Tokyo Toronto Warsaw

with associated companies in Berlin Ibadan

Oxford is a registered trade mark of Oxford University Press
in the UK and in certain other countries

ISBN 0 19 831470 1

Assembled by Ian Foulis & Associates, Plymouth, Devon
Printed by Cambridge University Press

Contents

Fiction

Poetry

Introduction to the Teacher

Oxford Literacy Skills Book 2 is the second book of a three-book 'skills programme', which aims to improve your students' literacy skills between the ages of 11 and 14.

We have deliberately designed this book as a flexible resource. We know from our own experience as English teachers that the most useful classroom resources are the ones teachers – and students – can dip into easily. Although this book is divided into units, each unit contains freestanding activity packages – focusing on:

- grammar and language skills
- comprehension
- extended responses to texts
- speaking and listening
- comparison of two contrasting texts
- extended writing.

If you wanted, and if time allowed, you could start at the beginning of each unit and work your way through – but at the same time it is possible to pick out just those skills you want to work on. (Each unit follows the same broad pattern of activities, to make selection easier.) For instance, you might guide your students through the grammar and language work, ask them to work individually on the comprehension activities, then form groups or pairs for a speaking and listening activity. Alternatively, you might want to concentrate on comprehension and extended writing assignments. You might have time to look at two texts, or you might instead prefer to focus on only one. The choice is yours.

All activities – with the obvious exception of Speaking and Listening tasks – have been phrased to allow for some sort of written outcome. However, you may prefer to use the language or comparison questions as class discussion activities, and then allow students to produce written answers for other activities. Certainly, many students coming up from Key Stage 2 will be used to 'shared', collaborative work on grammar and language, and you may want to extend this style of teaching into your language lessons in Key Stage 3. Our aim has been to leave as many options open to you and your students as possible.

We have also produced a series of Writing Frames – photocopiable sheets which will support your students as they work through these activities. You can download these, free of charge, from the website www.oup.co.uk/oxliteracyskills. Lastly, answers to all of the language, comprehension, and comparison questions appear in the photocopiable Answer Book which accompanies this Students' Book.

We have enjoyed putting this book together; we hope that you, and your students, enjoy using it.

Geoff Barton
Richard Broomhead
Fiona Edwards
Julie Macey

Non-fiction and media
Reporting disasters

Aims

In this unit you will:
- study how a tabloid newspaper report is structured
- examine how language and style are used in disaster reportage
- compare a newspaper report and a famous pre-1914 diary entry
- understand how one text can be more personal than another
- take part in a class debate on news reporting.

Language focus

When structuring a newspaper report the writer has to decide:
- how to set the report out
- what sort of language and style to use.

Presentational devices

Newspaper reporters organize a story by using **presentational devices**. These include:
- a headline (usually snappy and lively to grab the reader's attention)
- a strapline (sub-heading)
- a topic sentence (gives a summary of the whole story – usually in bold and focusing on who/what/where/when/why – known as the 'five Ws')
- short paragraphs
- text in columns
- quotations or comments from other people (in speech marks)

- pictures or diagrams
- captions (to explain what the picture is about or to link it to part of the story).

Language

Different types of reports use different types of language.
In disaster reports you tend to find:

- compressed language (such as in the headline) – for example 'Towns torn up in tornado horror'
- repetition (where language is repeated for effect)
- dramatic language to suit the content of the report (words such as 'shocked', 'crisis', etc.)
- words, phrases and active verbs to create a fast-moving pace (to keep the report lively and the reader interested. Look out for language such as 'hurtled', 'shot towards', 'bolted', 'plunged' and so on to add pace and tension.)
- simple, clear and understandable language which might seem more like spoken English rather than written (to make it informal) – for example 'Locals reckon the clear up will cost a packet.'
- use of the past tense (because the event has usually already taken place)
- a personal tone (the writer may reveal what he or she thinks by using highly-loaded words such as 'evil' and 'heartbreaking').

HE'S HUGE, HE'S POWERFUL HE'S FAST AND HE'S MEAN

Two million flee from Hurricane Floyd

From ANDY LINES
in Cocoa Beach, Florida

THOUSANDS of terrified British holidaymakers fled Florida last night as monster Hurricane Floyd headed towards them.

They were among nearly 2 million people ordered to quit homes and hotels in the biggest evacuation ever.

'Hurricane Floyd is huge, he's powerful, he's fast and he's mean,' said Richard Moore, public safety boss in North Carolina – also on its path.

'This is the sort of hurricane you have nightmares about,' said Bill O'Brien, emergency chief in Palm Beach County.

The storm, TWICE the size of Britain and expected to reach Category Five – the most powerful possible – could strike this morning. Its 155mph winds bringing 20ft waves and massive floods to Florida, Georgia and the Carolinas. Experts fear 'catastrophe' if it hits a heavily populated area.

And just days behind is Hurricane Gert, following a near identical path. 'It's terrifying,' said Debby Campbell, 27, of Bath, Somerset, in Miami Beach with pal Lisa Shepherd.

The girls, who are staying put, were assigned a ground floor cupboard padded with mattresses as an emergency shelter and were stock-piling bottled water, candles, medical supplies and tinned food.

Lisa, 26, said: 'If the hurricane doesn't get us we might be hit by the floods. If we go to a higher floor to escape that we are at risk from the wind. It seems there's no safe place to hide.'

Brits were also moved to safety as Floyd savaged the Bahamas with 155mph winds and 10in of rain.

Kevin Gater, 30, planned to marry Samantha Robinson, 23, there on Friday but they are sheltering on the fourth floor ballroom of their hotel near the capital Nassau. 'The wedding was to be in a gazebo on the beach but I don't suppose that will still be standing,' said Kevin, of Stoke, Staffs.

Best man Robert Owen, 27, also there with wife, Susanne, 27, said: 'There is flooding on the lower floors, waves are crashing in off the beach right up to the ground floor, trees have been ripped up and are lying on the roads.'

BIRD watchers are flocking to Rosehearty village in north Scotland following sightings of a rare short-billed dowitcher blown across the Atlantic by the hurricane.

NO CHANCE: Shopkeeper in Florida sprays defiant message on barricade

MONSTER: Satellite picture shows storm's terrifying size as it heads ashore

TEXT A

Tabloid newspapers are small in format, which makes them easy to handle. They have many images and eye-catching layout features, and are written in a lively style. This report from *The Mirror* looks at Hurricane Floyd, which raged through the USA in September

HE'S HUGE, HE'S POWERFUL HE'S FAST AND HE'S MEAN

Two million flee from Hurricane Floyd

NO CHANCE: Shopkeeper in Florida sprays defiant message on barricade

MONSTER: Satellite picture shows storm's terrifying size as it heads ashore

From ANDY LINES
in Cocoa Beach, Florida

THOUSANDS of terrified British holidaymakers fled Florida last night as monster Hurricane Floyd headed towards them.

They were among nearly 2 million people ordered to quit homes and hotels in the biggest evacuation ever.

'Hurricane Floyd is huge, he's powerful, he's fast and he's mean,' said Richard Moore, public safety boss in North Carolina – also on its path.

'This is the sort of hurricane you have nightmares about,' said Bill O'Brien, emergency chief in Palm Beach County.

The storm, TWICE the size of Britain and expected to reach Category Five – the most powerful possible – could strike this morning, its 155mph winds bringing 20ft waves and massive floods to Florida, Georgia and the Carolinas. Experts fear 'catastrophe' if it hits a heavily populated area.

And just days behind is Hurricane Gert, following a near identical path. 'It's terrifying,' said Debby Campbell, 27, of Bath, Somerset, in Miami Beach with pal Lisa Shepherd.

The girls, who are staying put, were assigned a ground floor cupboard padded with mattresses as an emergency shelter and were stock-piling bottled water, candles, medical supplies and tinned food.

Lisa, 26, said: 'If the hurricane doesn't get us we might be hit by the floods. If we go to a higher floor to escape that we are at risk from the wind. It seems there's no safe place to hide.'

Brits were also moved to safety as Floyd savaged the Bahamas with 155mph winds and 10in of rain.

Kevin Gater, 30, planned to marry Samantha Robinson, 23, there on Friday but they are sheltering on the fourth floor ballroom of their hotel near the capital Nassau. 'The wedding was to be in a gazebo on the beach but I don't suppose that will still be standing,' said Kevin, of Stoke, Staffs.

Best man Robert Owen, 27, also there with wife, Susanne, 27, said: 'There is flooding on the lower floors, waves are crashing in off the beach right up to the ground floor, trees have been ripped up and are lying on the roads.'

● **BIRD** watchers are flocking to Rosehearty village in north Scotland following sightings of a rare short-billed dowitcher blown across the Atlantic by the hurricane.

WORD BANK

assigned given
catastrophe a great and sudden disaster
defiant rebellious
evacuation removal of people from a dangerous place

gazebo a summer house or canopy/tent
identical exactly the same
stockpiling building up a reserve supply

Language questions

 Look at the diagram below – a blank plan of the newspaper report. Where would you place these presentational devices? Match them up.

Captions	
Columns	
Headline	
Strapline	
Topic sentence	
Picture/diagram	

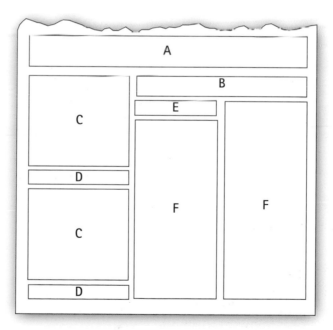

 Look at the article's headline.
How is repetition used to create suspense and drama?
What is the effect of a bold font and capital letters?
Write a short paragraph explaining your ideas in your own words.

 The writer uses dramatic language to show how frightening the situation is and to build up a sense of drama in the report. What picture does the reader form? Look at the examples below. Then find five more of your own and explain what ideas they conjure up.

Dramatic language	Picture it gives to the reader
Terrified	People were really scared.
Ordered to quit	This sounds like a desperate situation: 'ordered' sounds official and threatening, and 'to quit' seems final.

 The writer personifies Hurricane Floyd (makes it seem human) through his choice of verbs, to give a really clear image. Look at this example and then find two more on your own.

Hurricane Floyd headed towards them

List your findings, and then explain in one or two sentences why you think the writer chooses to use this technique here.

 Look at these two examples of reportage.
a) The car went out of control and hit a tree.
b) The stolen car hurtled out of control, collided with a passing cyclist and smashed into a heavy oak tree.

The first example is very vague and tells the reader little about what happened. However, the second example gives more detail about the event, telling the reader that the car is 'stolen' and the tree is a 'heavy oak'. It uses more animated language such as 'hurtled', 'collided' and 'smashed', giving a real sense of speed, power, and danger.

Make this paragraph more active and dramatic by adding more detail.

Yesterday, an earthquake occurred in South America. Several hundred people were injured and buildings were damaged. An earthquake like this has not happened before in this area.

These prompts might help you add to this:
▶ Was the earthquake expected?
▶ How violent was it?

▶ How were people hurt?

▶ What state were the buildings in?

Read your new version to someone else. Do they think it is more dramatic and lively? Explain what they said about your version in a sentence.

Comprehension

1 Look at the topic sentence below.

THOUSANDS of terrified British holidaymakers fled Florida last night as monster Hurricane Floyd headed towards them.

Fill in the grid below to check whether the sentence really does include the five Ws.

Who?	
What?	
Where?	
When?	
Why?	

2 How do you know that this is the worst hurricane to hit Florida?
Hint Look in paragraph 2.

3 Explain how enormous the hurricane is. Give exact details.

4 What are the girls from Bath doing to protect themselves?

5 Why is Kevin Gater not hopeful about his coming wedding?

6 Look at the pictures which accompany the article. Why do you think the shopkeeper is spraying a message on the barricade to his shop?

7 The report mentions damage that Hurricane Floyd has caused. Give two examples.

8 Based on the report as a whole, explain in a sentence what picture you have formed of the hurricane and the situation in America.

Extended response

How would you describe the writer's style in this report?

▶ Journalistic? (Does it sound like a newspaper report?)
▶ Dramatic? (Look back at Language questions 3 and 4.)
▶ Thoughtful? (Does the writer reflect upon the events?)
▶ Too sensational and over the top? (Does the style and use of language get in the way of telling the reader the basic story?)

Write an extended paragraph, giving examples to support your thoughts. (Refer back to your answers to the Language questions.)

This question is asking for a personal response to the text. This means that your teacher is not expecting a specific answer – he or she wants to see what you think.

Speaking and listening

Class and small groups

How far is it acceptable for the media to report on disasters that impact on other peoples' lives?

Disasters often feature as high-profile news even if they are in remote parts of the world. Get into small groups of four or five and think about these questions:

▶ Why do we like to hear about disasters?
▶ What might we learn from them?
▶ How realistic do you think the news is that we receive?

▶ Is it fair to show people's suffering?
▶ Can disaster reporting be a benefit to those who might be in trouble?

Make notes on what your group thinks and remember that the task is to decide how acceptable it is to report on disasters. You will then join together as a whole class to discuss this issue. Be prepared for everyone in the group to say something.

TEXT B

Samuel Pepys (1633-1703) was a civil servant working for Charles II during the 1660s. At this time he kept an informal, honest record of his private and public life giving us a vivid picture of England at that time. He wrote in shorthand which was not deciphered until 1825 and his diaries were not published in full until 1970. The real diaries still exist and are housed in Magdalene College, Cambridge, where Pepys studied.

The Fire of London, 2 September 1666

September 2 1666 Lords day. Some of our maids sitting up late last night to get things ready against our feast today, Jane called us up, about 3 in the morning, to tell us of a great fire they saw in the City. So I rose, and slipped on my nightgown and went to her window, and thought it to be on the back side of Markelane at the furthest; but being unused to such fires as fallowed, I thought it far enough off, and so went to bed again and to sleep. About 7 rose again to dress myself, and there looked out at the window and saw the fire not so much as it was, and further off. So to my closet to set things to rights after yesterday's cleaning. By and by Jane comes and tells me that she hears that above 300 houses have been burned down tonight by the fire we saw, and that it was now burning down all Fishstreet by London Bridge. So I made myself ready presently, and walked to the Tower and there got up upon one of the high places, Sir J. Robinsons little son going up with me; and there I did see the houses at that end of the bridge all on fire, and an infinite great fire on this and the other side the end of the bridge - which, among other people, did trouble me for poor little Michell and our Sarah on the Bridge. So down, with my heart full of trouble, to the Lieutenant of the Tower, who tells me that it begun this morning in the King's bakers house in Pudding-lane, and that it hath burned down St Magnes Church and most part of Fishstreete already. So I down to the water-side and there got a boat and through bridge, and there saw a lamentable fire. Poor Michells house, as far as the Old Swan, already burned that way and the fire running further, that in a very little time it got as far as the Stillyard while I was there. Everybody endeavouring to remove their goods, and flinging into the River or bringing them into lighters that lay off. Poor people staying in their houses as long as till the very fire touched them, and then running into boats or clambering from one pair of stair by the water-side to another. And among other things, the poor pigeons I perceive were loath to leave their houses, but hovered about the windows and balconies till they were some of them burned, their wings, and fell down.

Having stayed, and in an hour's time seen the fire rage every way, and nobody to my sight endeavouring to quench it, but to remove their goods and leave all to the fire; and having seen it get as far as the Steeleyard,

and the wind mighty high and driving it into the city, and everything, after so long a drougth, proving combustible, even the very stones of churches, and among other things, the poor steeple by which pretty Mrs Horsley lives, and whereof my old school-fellow Elborough is parson, taken fire in the very top and there burned till it fall down - I to White-hall with a gentleman with me who desired to go off from the Tower to see the fire in my boat - to White-hall, and there up to the King's closet in the chapel, where people came about me and I did give them an account dismayed them all; and word was carried in to the King, so I was called for and did tell the King and Duke of York what I saw, and that unless his Majesty did command houses to be pulled down, nothing could stop the fire. They seemed much troubled, and the King commanded me to go to my Lord Mayor from him and command him to spare no houses but to pull down before the fire every way. The Duke of York bid me tell him that if he would have any more soldiers, he shall; and so did my Lord Arlington afterward, as a great secret. Here meeting with Captain Cocke, I in his coach, which he lent me, and Creed with me, to Pauls; and there walked along Watling-street as well as I could, every creature coming away loaden with goods to save - and here and there sick people carried away in beds. Extraordinary good goods carried in carts and on backs. At last met my Lord Mayor in Canning Streete, like a man spent, with a hankercher about his neck. To the King's message, he cried like a fainting woman, 'Lord, what can I do? I am spent. People will not obey me. I have been pulling down houses. But the fire overtakes us faster then we can do it.'

Samuel Pepys

WORD BANK

by and by then	**hankercher** handkerchief	**presently** at once
closet a private room	**infinite** great, endless	**quench** put out
combustible capable of burning	**lamentable** regrettable	**spent** exhausted
dismayed upset	**lighters** small boats	**whereof** of which
endeavouring trying hard	**loath to** unwilling to	
fallowed followed	**perceive** observe, understand	

Comparison

 1 Why did Samuel Pepys go back to bed after seeing the fire from the window?

 2 When and where did the fire start?

3 What is happening to make the fire worse?
(**Hint**) Look at the start of the second paragraph.

 4 Pepys' diary was not written to be read by other people. We can tell this because his way of writing is informal, almost chatty; more like spoken English.
Find an example to support this and explain why you chose it.
(**Hint**) Look at how he starts sentences with 'so'.

5 How does Pepys make his writing dramatic?
a) Find four dramatic sentences in Text B.
b) What makes these sentences dramatic? Is it:
   ▶ the language Pepys uses?
   ▶ the events he describes?
c) Compare this with Text A. Do the two texts produce drama in the same or different ways?
   (**Hint**) Look at your answers to Language questions 3 and 4.

 6 A diary is a personal record of a life. It differs from a newspaper report as it is more personal, honest and written from the writer's point of view (more opinions than fact). It also has a more emotional feel to it.
a) Which of these examples from Texts A and B could be described as personal?

Extracts	Personal (yes or no)
So I made myself ready presently (B)	
'This is the sort of hurricane you have nightmares about' (A)	
Did trouble me for poor little Michell (B)	
Begun this morning in the King's bakers house in Pudding-lane (B)	

'If the hurricane doesn't get us we might be hit by floods' (A)	
I did give them an account dismayed them all (B)	
Experts fear 'catastrophe' if it hits a heavily populated area (A)	
So down, with my heart full of trouble (B)	

b) How could you tell that certain examples were personal? Write a short explanation.

 The chart below shows you similarities and differences in the way both passages have been written.

Text A	Text B
Tabloid newspaper report (tabloids are known for their sensational and over-the-top style of writing)	Diary entry (usually not for public viewing)
General public audience	No specific audience (private)
Not objective here – the writer tries to affect our opinion of the situation	Not objective, as it is his thoughts and ideas ('I' is used throughout to show this)
The writer is a professional who is not involved in the situation he is describing.	The writer is inside the situation he is describing, and knows the people affected.
Written to report and inform	Written to reflect and record

Look at the grid above and your answers to the other Comparison questions. Based on these, answer these questions and give an explanation for each point:

▶ Which writer is trying to make events seem most dramatic?
▶ Which writer is most emotionally involved with what is happening?
▶ Which text has a definite audience and a specific purpose?
▶ Whose writing can we rely on the most?

Writing assignments

1 Write a tabloid newspaper report on the Great Fire of London. You might need to do some additional research about London in the 1660s and the fire itself. In your report remember to:

- use appropriate presentational devices to structure your work (look at the Language focus on pages 6-7 for a reminder of these)
- use a combination of sentence types to keep your audience interested
- begin with a topic sentence (remember the five Ws)
- think about language features (look back at the Language focus section, and remember to use active verbs and dramatic language)
- use Samuel Pepys' words as eyewitness accounts or in an interview in the article
- remember to remain neutral and not give your opinions.

2 One of the girls from Text A decides to use her experience of the hurricane as part of her autobiography. Imagine that you are the girl. What would you write? (Remember to use the first person singular 'I', as it is from your point of view as the girl.)

Think about:
- which part of the storm to focus on (its approach? the main storm? the aftermath) – don't try to cover all parts, aim to focus on one
- making your writing really detailed and interesting
- a gripping opening to interest the reader
- using dramatic language and vocabulary to build up a sense of danger (look back at the Language focus section on p7 to remind yourself)
- giving the reader a picture of what the hurricane is like (the writer used personification in the tabloid report) - think about using similes and metaphors (comparisons to help the reader see what is happening, e.g. 'the wind tugged at buildings like an angry child seeking its mother's attention'

Non-fiction and media
Letter by letter

In this unit you will:
- examine a media campaign letter and a personal one
- learn how to set out different kinds of letters
- see how tone and style depend on audience and purpose
- compare and contrast letter styles
- analyse and use techniques to improve your letter-writing style.

Language focus

Letters have always been an important form of communication. We tend to use two main styles:
- formal (business letters, job application letters, etc.)
- informal (letters to friends and family).

Rules for layout of letters

Formal style

> Your address
>
> Write the date in full

The addressee's name
Their title/position
The address

Dear Mr or Ms Surname
or Dear Sir/Madam

Subject of letter

I am writing ...

Write the letter in a formal style

Yours sincerely – *if you know their name*
Yours faithfully – *if you wrote Dear Sir*

> Your name

Informal style

> Your address
>
> Today's date

Dear first name

Write your letter in an informal style

Best wishes, *or*
See you soon *or*
All the best

> Your first name

Features of persuasive letters

Media campaigns use some kinds of letters too. They are laid out like normal letters, but their style is much more informative and persuasive. Some key features of campaign letters are outlined here:

Rhetorical questions

This is when the writer asks a question not for information but to produce an effect on the reader. For example 'who cares?' means 'nobody cares'. Watch out for these in persuasive texts.

Persuasive/Emotional style

In order to persuade us to do something, writers often appeal to our emotions or try to gain our sympathy. They can do this by:

▶ telling an individual story rather than talking in general terms (e.g. 'Toddler Ben slipped and fell down the stairs when his mum's back was turned' gets your attention and sympathy more than 'unsupervised children can easily fall downstairs')

▶ using specific words and phrases to tell the reader how to feel (e.g. 'Poor Ben suffered a painful broken leg and a nasty black eye', rather than 'Ben broke a leg and got a black eye')

▶ giving detailed information (e.g. 'Ben bounced down seven stairs and crashed into the table in the hall' rather than 'Ben fell downstairs')

▶ including a picture to grab the reader's attention and make them react (actually seeing Ben's injuries might make the reader feel more sorry for him, and more determined to do something about the situation).

Repetition

Writers may repeat words and phrases in order to create an effect, and to remind the reader of key ideas and points.

Imperative

The imperative is the command form of the verb. Writers use it to give an order or direct instruction such as 'Be quiet', 'Sit down', or 'Write to this address now'.

Person of the verb

There are three classes of person in speech and writing: first person, second person and third person:

	Singular	Plural
First person	I	We
Second person	You	You (more than one)
Third person	He/she/it	They

First person singular 'I want to tell you about the work of the RSPCA.'
'I' makes the sentence sound personal, direct, and immediate.

First person plural 'We want to help as many animals as possible.'
'We' makes it sound like a group or company is speaking, suggesting that more than one person is involved.

Second person singular and plural 'Your help will make all the difference.'
'Your' is directly addressing the reader and seems more personal.

Third person singular and plural 'He was critically ill', 'Their lives are at risk.'
'He' and 'Their' are less personal but let the writer make the text almost into a story.

▷ Lists of three:
e.g. smoking is expensive①, antisocial② and bad for your health③.

TEXT A

This letter was written by the RSPCA to persuade people to donate money to continue the work done by the charity. The letter focuses on three kittens and their mother.

The style of writing is formal, but designed to affect the reader's emotions, so they will give money.

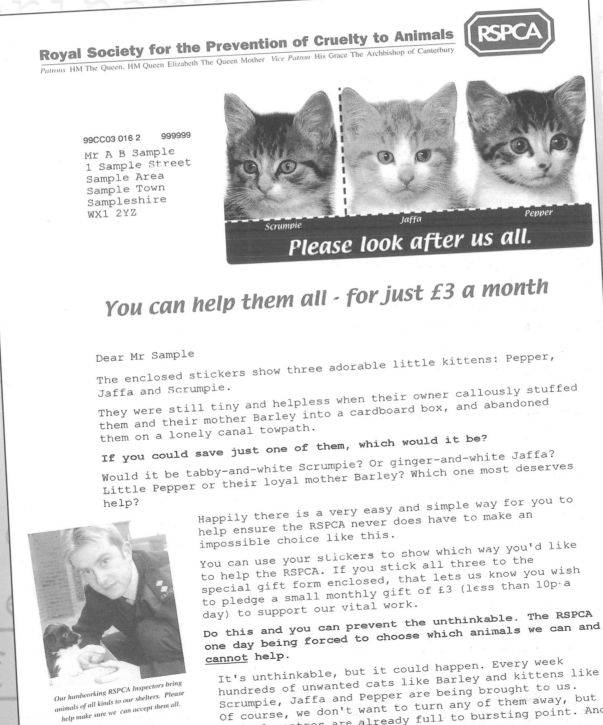

Royal Society for the Prevention of Cruelty to Animals RSPCA

Patrons HM The Queen, HM Queen Elizabeth The Queen Mother *Vice Patron* His Grace The Archbishop of Canterbury

99CC03 016 2   999999
Mr A B Sample
1 Sample Street
Sample Area
Sample Town
Sampleshire
WX1 2YZ

Scrumpie   *Jaffa*   *Pepper*

Please look after us all.

You can help them all - for just £3 a month

Dear Mr Sample

The enclosed stickers show three adorable little kittens: Pepper, Jaffa and Scrumpie.

They were still tiny and helpless when their owner callously stuffed them and their mother Barley into a cardboard box, and abandoned them on a lonely canal towpath.

If you could save just one of them, which would it be?

Would it be tabby-and-white Scrumpie? Or ginger-and-white Jaffa? Little Pepper or their loyal mother Barley? Which one most deserves help?

Happily there is a very easy and simple way for you to help ensure the RSPCA never does have to make an impossible choice like this.

You can use your stickers to show which way you'd like to help the RSPCA. If you stick all three to the special gift form enclosed, that lets us know you wish to pledge a small monthly gift of £3 (less than 10p a day) to support our vital work.

Do this and you can prevent the unthinkable. The RSPCA one day being forced to choose which animals we can and <u>cannot</u> help.

Our hardworking RSPCA Inspectors bring animals of all kinds to our shelters. Please help make sure we can accept them all.

It's unthinkable, but it could happen. Every week hundreds of unwanted cats like Barley and kittens like Scrumpie, Jaffa and Pepper are being brought to us. Of course, we don't want to turn any of them away, but our animal centres are already full to bursting point. And we are a charity. We get no help from the government.

PTO...

00000447

The RSPCA currently rehomes <u>almost 100,000</u> animals a year – far more than any other animal welfare organisation. And whilst we are searching for suitable homes for them all, these animals need food, shelter, veterinary treatment, and plenty of love to restore their trust in humans. To stop the problem getting even bigger, we also make sure every cat and dog that leaves us is neutered and microchipped; that alone can cost anything from £40 – £60 per animal.

So you can see it takes a great deal of money to give every animal the care and treatment it needs. The pets' new owners do make a contribution, but often it's only a fraction of what we've spent. <u>To make up the difference we are totally dependent on the kindness and generosity of our supporters.</u>

Just £3 a month helps make sure <u>no animal is left out.</u>

Regular gifts let us plan ahead, knowing that we can rely on your monthly donation to help us accept <u>every</u> animal that needs our care. So if you can, **please reply in the next 14 days.** We never want to have to choose between animals like Scrumpie, Jaffa, and Pepper.

Please help make sure we don't have to. Attach <u>all</u> your stickers to the <u>standing order</u> form enclosed with this letter to support our vital work with a regular gift now.

Thank you.

Yours sincerely,

[signature]

Anthony Baumann
Head of Fundraising

PS In the event, we didn't have to choose between Pepper, Jaffa and Scrumpie. All three kittens and their mother Barley were lovingly cared for by RSPCA staff until permanent new homes were found for them. Your regular gift can help give more animals this same chance.

photos © RSPCA unless indicated

WORD BANK

callously unfeelingly
neutered operated on so they will not have young
standing order form a form that tells your bank to pay regular amounts to someone

Language questions

 1 How can you tell that this is a letter? Pick out three reasons.
Hint Use the two letter style examples to help you.

 2 This letter uses some presentational (layout) features, which you would not expect to find in a formal or informal letter. Find two.
Hint Look at techniques used to focus our attention.

 3 The writer has used several rhetorical questions in the letter. Find two of them. Then try to explain how you think these questions aim to persuade the reader.

 4 The style of the letter is emotionally persuasive throughout. Find five examples of phrases or sentences that are designed to affect the reader's emotions. Write them in the example column and then explain the possible effect of the language on the reader.

Example	Effect
Tiny and helpless when their owner callously	'tiny and helpless' suggests they are small and weak and need helping; 'callously' shows that they have been treated badly

 5 The writer uses repetition (see Language focus) in the letter. See if you can find two examples of repetition and then try to say why the writer uses this technique.
Hint Look at how the writer keeps referring to the reader and the kittens.

 6 a) Which person of the verb is used to refer to the RSPCA?
Hint Look back at the language focus section.
b) How does this show that the RSPCA is a community of workers?

 7 Look at the end of paragraph eight. It ends with two simple sentences:

And we are a charity. We get no help from the government.

a) Why do you think the writer chose to alter the type of sentence here?

b) How might the use of simple sentences here help to stress the RSPCA's message? Do you think it works?

 8 The imperative form of the verb (command) is used at two points in the letter.

a) Find these examples.

b) Why does the writer use this form of the verb? Pick the best answer:
  ▶ The writer is bossy.
  ▶ The writer is trying to give simple and clear instructions about what to do.
  ▶ The writer thinks the reader needs guidance, as they might not understand.

 9 The style of the letter is partly what makes it successful. Which of these adjectives describe the style of the letter?
  ▶ positive
  ▶ persuasive
  ▶ serious
  ▶ hopeful
  ▶ miserable
  ▶ direct

For each one that you think does match the style of the letter, try to find evidence in the letter to support it.

Comprehension

 1 Paragraph nine is about the RSPCA and what it does to care for animals. List the sorts of things that it does.

 2 Look at the underlined part of paragraph ten. Pick out the two words used to praise people who help the RSPCA.

 3 Why do you think the writer chose to picture the three kittens and name them and their mother?

4 The letter says

> Happily there is a very easy and simple way for you to help.

Why would this persuade people to help?

5 How does the writer try to make out that your donation is not much money for you to part with? Pick out three words that are used.

6 What, in paragraph nine, shows that the RSPCA is very good at what it does?

7 What effect do you think the picture of the kitten behind bars would have on the reader? Why do you think this was included?

8 The letter ends with a PS which gives the story of Pepper, Jaffa, Scrumpie and Barley a happy ending. Do you think this is an effective way to end the letter?

Extended response

What image does the writer present of the RSPCA in this letter?

This question wants you to look at how the writer portrays the RSPCA; in other words the effect he has on the reader. Use the structure below to answer the question. Write a short paragraph for each point:

▶ How does the RSPCA seem to feel about the kittens and their mother? Pick out language to show this – look back at Language question 4.

▶ How does the RSPCA show you that your donation will be well spent? What sort of things does it do with the donations?

▶ What pressure does the writer suggest the RSPCA is under?

▶ How does the charity refer to you (as a potential donor)? Look at the language used.

> ▶ What use is made of pictures? Look in particular at the one with the Inspector.
> ▶ Why does the writer have to be positive and optimistic about the RSPCA throughout the letter?

Speaking and listening

Pairs

You have been commissioned to write the script for a new RSPCA advert for radio based on Text A. It will last for 30 seconds. You have to remember that your audience will only be able to hear and so you will have to work hard to create pictures in their heads if your campaign is going to be successful. In your advert you will need to:

- ▶ script what you are going to say
- ▶ explain what the RSPCA does
- ▶ use language to inform but more importantly to persuade

- ▶ use specific examples of animal cruelty to have an impact on your listener
- ▶ use the techniques from the letter (such as 'you' and 'your' to refer to the audience, the imperative to be direct, rhetorical questions to make your audience think, repetition to stress important points or give emphasis)
- ▶ give an address, contact number or email address
- ▶ decide whether to ask for a specific donation or leave it up to the listener
- ▶ think of using music, soft sound effects and silence to make create more effects.

TEXT B

● ●

This letter is still about cats but of a more serious and sinister nature.

Rosemary Rhodes lives on Bodmin Moor in Cornwall. This letter, to a friend, focuses on her strange encounters with a large cat or beast. Over a series of years Rosemary and her farm-hands had several experiences, usually involving livestock being killed and mutilated.

Withybrook Woods
St. Luke's End
Bodmin Moor
Cornwall
PL7 2YZ

December 1999

Dear Megan,

Thank you for your lovely card and long newsy letter. I can't believe another year has gone by so quickly. Such a lot has happened though. If you think life in the middle of Bodmin Moor is peaceful and uneventful, you may be about to change your mind.

It all started last winter when I began to find my sheep mutilated and dead, or worse still, mutilated and still alive. I was unwilling to blame the usual culprits, i.e. fox, badger or marauding pet dogs. The more I thought about it, the more I came to the conclusion that the wounds the poor things were suffering could not possibly have been inflicted by our native predators as they simply don't have the weapons.

Needless to say I was not taken at all seriously when I first started to question, publicly, what was happening here. Don Rogers (one of my farm workers) was even threatening to leave. He was getting a lot of teasing from the other farmers and farm workers who frankly thought I was loopy. He was definitely inclined to believe them.

This was until late one night during the winter when he and his eldest son, Antony, were out rabbiting. They were walking quietly with guns and carrying a one-million-candle-power lamp. As they crossed one of my top fields, soundlessly, with no light, they heard a most unusual yelping noise. When they shone their light in that direction, they saw a big dog fox, running for its life towards them from an enormous cat. They decided later when they had had a chance to look up a few books that it was a Puma. It was six foot long from nose to tail and a tawny sandy colour. The cat came to a grinding halt. It paused for a few seconds, allowing them to get a good sighting, before it turned and fled back to the forest.

Don and Antony arrived back in the farm kitchen at about 1am. They were very pale, very shaken and very certain that we have a big cat problem on Bodmin Moor (and that missus wasn't quite so barmy as they had thought). However this had started all of us really thinking and from then on we really kept our eyes open for signs. We found plenty.

We began to go out at night, looking for these animals with very high-powered lamps. We found that the cat's eyes reacted to the light in an incredible fashion. We already knew that at night all animals' eyes reflect differently. We could recognize the eyes of sheep, rabbit, cattle, dog, domestic cat, fox, badger or deer, but the cat's eyes were like great orbs of gold — instantly riveting and unlike anything we had seen before.

The local Police dog handler has seen the cat up here three or four times. One day I was telling him how Don could sometimes squeak the cat up. 'Squeaking up' is the term Cornishmen use to describe the noise they can make using their mouths on the back of their hands making the sound of a trapped or distressed rabbit. This is to lure the fox into range when we have been losing baby lambs to them in the spring.

Anyway, the constable duly arrived here late one evening and off we went, on foot towards the moor. Sure enough we soon picked up the eyes of the cat on the far moor boundary. We doused the lamp and Don started squeaking. A minute or so later we shone the lamp again and the eyes were shining from a hedge closer in. Another couple of minutes and it was only fifty yards from us in the bracken. Poor Peter just exploded and made off rapidly back to the house for his car which he drove back to us saying 'You aren't hunting that cat, the darned thing is hunting you.'

One hot evening this summer, I had a really close encounter. At dusk I went out to check the stock. As I carried an armful of hay into the yard, I called the cows much in the same fashion as men world-wide use to their stock — a long, yodelly come-on call. At once, from an open-sided Barn beside the beasts, a large Puma emerged. While I stood totally transfixed, the cattle panicked. Luckily they made for the far fence. Had they made for the only exit from the yard they would have trampled me as I was blocking it. The fence the cattle hit was about 4'6" high. The wire is square rigged underneath, which the cows climbed, with two rows of barbed wire on the top, which they straddled and fell over. Never, in all my life have I seen cattle behave so. I was appalled as the poor things could have ripped their udders to pieces on the barbs. So my first thought was to check them. Praise be, they were only scratched. Then I fell apart and legged it back to the house, fast, to phone Don at home for help. I have to tell you, Meg, I was scared. I shook for ages and didn't sleep too well either.

However the whole thing really got to my soul this autumn. I had had a couple of my sheep badly mutilated but not dead and I was having to call the vet out to put them down. This is really harrowing you know. The one that hurt the most was when my little Soay sheep went missing one evening

and was found alive with the usual horrific wounds to her abdomen. She was more of a pet really. How the cat managed to get her I don't know. I could never catch her. She was as wild as a hawk and could jump six foot from a standing start. I was beside myself and put her very carefully into the back of the Landrover and rushed her ten miles to Launceston to the vet in the hope that they could sew her up again. They very gently pointed out that her intestines had been trapped and that she would most certainly die of gangrene within a few days, so we put her down.

It went from bad to worse. I decided to bring them all in at night. We counted them out and we counted them in. Then I started losing them in the middle of the day within sight of the house. I was at this time in touch with the cat experts at London Zoo. They said this could be typical of leopards who tend to be opportunists. They prefer not to hunt in broad daylight but if there is no dinner available, they will take lunch. In the end I could stand it no longer and

I sold the lot. I'd had enough of being the fast food emporium to a bunch of felines!

One nice little footnote though. This summer Kate spent several months working in Africa for Botswana Telecom. So with fewer responsibilities, I flew out to stay with her. I had the time of my life. We stayed in three different countries, in three different Game reserves. I saw every animal under the sun. You name it, we saw it. That is, all except leopard. After our last trek, the young game warden was bemoaning the fact that he hadn't managed to show us a leopard. 'Oh, never mind,' I said airily, 'we've plenty of those at home.' Are you likely to be able to come to see me this year? Please try. I could take you on a Safari all of our own.

Much love

Rosemary

WORD BANK

bemoaning lamenting, regretting
culprits villains, suspects
doused put out
emporium a big shop like a department store
felines animals of the cat family
gangrene a disease where flesh rots

lure attract (usually with bait)
mutilated horribly wounded
marauding raiding with the object of stealing
native local
opportunists out for what they can get
orbs spheres

predators animals that eat others
riveting attention-grabbing
straddled tried to cross
transfixed terrified and unable to move

Comparison

 1 According to Rosemary, what sort of creatures <u>usually</u> attack her sheep?

2 What persuaded Don Rogers that Rosemary might be telling him the truth after all?

3 When Rosemary saw the cat in her barn, how did she react?

 **4** What eventually forced her to sell all her sheep?

5 This letter is very different from Text A as it is informal and personal, rather than persuasive. Look at the chart below and looking again at the letter, find an example to support each technique:

Style category	Example from letter
Use of informal language	
Use of dialect (language only used in certain areas of the country)	
Direct approach to reader using pronoun 'you'	
Use of humour	
Use of questions	
Sentences that sound more like conversation	
Friendly tone	
Use of first person singular	

 6 Although both letters are different in style, they use similar techniques in gaining our interest very quickly. Look at the bold headline at the start of Text A and the first paragraph of Text B. How do these devices make us interested? Write a short explanation.

 7 Look at both letters. Which one is:

- most persuasive?
- most detailed and informative?
- most reliable and honest?
- more like speech than writing?

- most revealing about the writer as a person?
- most formal in style?
- least formal in style?
- friendliest in its tone?

For each example above write a sentence to explain your ideas. Back up your ideas with clear reference to the letters.

Writing assignments

1 Imagine that you are Rosemary Rhodes in Text B and write to your local MP to ask for help with the large cat situation. Remember that this is a formal letter so you need to:

▷ set it out formally (like the plan in the Language focus on p19) as you want to be taken seriously

▷ explain why you are writing and describe the situation

▷ say how it has made you feel

▷ suggest outcomes, solutions to the situation and the sort of help you need

▷ use language to persuade your reader (as you want help, remember!) – look at p20 to remind yourself of persuasive language you can use.

2 Design a campaign leaflet from the RSPCA, aimed at teenagers. The leaflet should provide information and persuade its readers that pets should not be given as presents at Christmas.
In your writing, remember to:

▷ write for your own age group: keep it friendly, informal and lively – don't be afraid to use slang and the sort of English that you would use more in speech

▷ think of a suitable heading or title

▷ set out your leaflet to gain maximum impact – think about using colour, boxes and borders, bold, italics and underlinings, images and diagrams, headings and subheadings to organize points, bullets to shorten the text

▷ give reasons why giving pets as presents can be a problem

▷ perhaps tell a story about one person's or animal's situation to make the reader understand your point of view (like the story of the kittens in Text A).

Although you are writing a leaflet, not a letter, remember to look back at the Language focus on p20 and use the persuasive devices described there.

Non-fiction and media

Tense: nervous?

Aims

In this unit you will:

▶ learn about tenses and regular and irregular verbs and their patterns

▶ look at how tenses are used in different kinds of text and how they can be used for effect

▶ compare an autobiographical account with a scene from a television script, looking at how writers present characters

▶ devise a new script for a TV comedy or write a diary cntry.

Language focus

A verb is a doing word. It gives action to a sentence. It might inform us about what people or things do, have done or are going to do. Verbs change their form to show time: whether the sentence relates to the past, the present or the future. We call this the verb tense. For example:

I did my homework last night – **Past tense**
I am doing my homework – **Present tense**
I will do my homework later – **Future tense**

Verbs fall into two categories – regular and irregular.

Regular verbs
Most verbs are regular - they all obey the same rules. For example:

Infinitive (verb in original state)	Present tense (happening now)	Past tense (already happened)	Participles (ing or ed)	Future (yet to happen)
To cook	I cook You cook He/she/it cooks We cook They cook	cooked	cooking (present) cooked (past)	will cook shall cook going to cook

Regular verbs follow this pattern in the present tense, adding **s** to the third person singular (he/she/it form). However, some regular verbs do change slightly. Look at this chart to see what happens:

Infinitive	Third person singular
To try	He/she/it tr**ies**

You can see that the he/she/it form changes in this case. You can probably think of others.

We usually form the past tense of regular verbs by adding **ed** to the infinitive ('cook' becomes 'cooked'.) However, be careful as there are again some special cases:

Infinitive	Present tense	Past tense
To imagine	I imagine	I imagine**d**
To cry	I cry	I cr**ied**

Here, as 'imagine' ends in an **e**, you just add **d** – but in 'cry' you have to drop the **y** and add **ied**.

Irregular verbs

There are many verbs which do not follow the pattern outlined above. We call these irregular verbs. It is more difficult to remember the formation of irregular verbs, and there is no easy way except to learn these as we come across them, but we can detect patterns within groups of irregular verbs. The most commonly used irregular verbs in English are shown on the next page:

Infinitive (verb in original state)	Present tense (happening now)	Past tense (already happened)	Participles	Future (yet to happen)
To be	I am You are He/she/it is We are They are	was were	being been	will be shall be going to be
To have	I have You have He/she/it has We have They have	had	having had	will have shall have going to have

There are some other awkward irregular verbs shown in the grid below:

Infinitive (verb in original state)	Present tense (happening now)	Past tense (already happened)	Past participle
To learn	I learn	I learnt	learnt
To sleep	I sleep	I slept	slept

You have probably spotted that verbs with **ea** in the middle, like 'l**ea**rn', add a letter **t** to form the past tense. Similarly, verbs with **ee** in the middle, like 'sl**ee**p', drop one letter **e** and add **pt**. You can probably think of other verbs that follow this pattern. You will be focusing on other irregular verbs in this unit.

The only way to spot if a verb is regular or irregular is to look at it in the past tense and see how it changes. In the past tense many irregular verbs change dramatically, but if you know the patterns, the verbs are not hard to recognize.

TEXT A

Laurie Lee was born and brought up in Gloucestershire, England. His famous book *Cider with Rosie* is autobiographical and deals with his childhood experiences in the village of Slad. In this extract Laurie Lee looks back on his early school days, in particular on the tyrant teacher known by the children as Crabby. Autobiographical writing tends to focus on the writer's recollections of his or her life and is normally written in the past tense.

Cider with Rosie

SHE WAS A BUNCHED AND PUNITIVE LITTLE BODY and the school had christened her Crabby; she had a sour yellow look, lank hair coiled in earphones, and the skin and voice of a turkey. We were all afraid of the gobbling Miss B; she spied, she pried, she crouched, she crept, she pounced – she was a terror.

Each morning was war without declaration; no one knew who would catch it next. We stood to attention, half-crippled in our desks, till Miss B walked in, whacked the walls with a ruler, and fixed us with her squinting eye. 'Good a-morning, children!' 'Good morning, Teacher!' The greeting was like a rattling of swords. Then she would scowl at the floor and begin to growl 'Ar Farther...'; at which we said the Lord's Prayer, praised all good things, and thanked God for the health of our King. But scarcely had we bellowed the last Amen than Crabby coiled, uncoiled, and sprang, and knocked some poor boy sideways.

One seldom knew why; one was always off guard, for the punishment preceded the charge. The charge, however, followed hard upon it, to a light shower of angry spitting.

'Shuffling your feet! Playing with the desk! A-smirking at that miserable Betty! I will not have it. I'll not, I say. I repeat – I will not have it!'

Many a punch-drunk boy in a playground battle, out-numbered and beaten to his knees, would be heard to cry: 'I will not have it! I'll not, I say! I repeats I will not have it!' It was an appeal to the code of our common suffering, and called for immediate mercy.

So we did not much approve of Crabby – though she was responsible for our excellent reflexes. Apart from this, her teaching was not memorable. She appears in my recollection as merely a militant figure, a hunched-up little creature all spring-coils and slaps – not a monster by any means, but a natural manifestation of what we expected of school.

For school in my day, that day, Crabby's day, seemed to be designed simply to keep

us out of the air and from following the normal pursuits of the fields. Crabby's science of dates and sums and writing seemed a typical invention of her own, a sour form of fiddling or prison-labour like picking oakum or sewing sacks.

So while the bright times passed, we sat locked in our stocks, our bent backs turned on the valley. The June air infected us with primitive hungers, grass-seed and thistle-down idled through the windows, we smelt the fields and were tormented by cuckoos, while every out-of-door sound that came drifting in was a sharp nudge in the solar plexus. The creaking of wagons going past the school, harness-jingle, and the cries of the carters, the calling of cows from the 17-Acre, Fletcher's chattering mower, gunshots from the warrens – all tugged and pulled at our active wishes till we could have done Miss B a murder.

And indeed there came the inevitable day when rebellion raised its standard, when the tension was broken and a hero emerged whom we would willingly have named streets after. At least, from that day his name was honoured, though we gave him little support at the time…

Spadge Hopkins it was, and I must say we were surprised. He was one of those heavy, full-grown boys, thick-legged, red-fisted, bursting with flesh, designed for the great outdoors. He was nearly fourteen by then, and physically out of scale – at least so far as our school was concerned. The sight of him squeezed into his tiny desk was worse than a bullock in ballet-shoes. He wasn't much of a scholar; he groaned as he worked, or hacked at his desk with a jack-knife. Miss B took her pleasure in goading him, in forcing him to read out loud; or asking him sudden unintelligible questions which made him flush and stumble.

The great day came; a day of shimmering summer, with the valley outside in a state of leafy levitation. Crabby B was at her sourest, and Spadge Hopkins had had enough. He began to writhe in his desk, and roll his eyes, and kick with his boots, and mutter; 'She'd better look out. 'Er, – Crabby B. She'd better, that's all. I can tell you…'

We didn't quite know what the matter was, in spite of his meaning looks. Then he threw down his pen, said; 'Sod it all,' got up, and walked to the door.

'And where are you going, young man, may I ask?' said Crabby with her awful leer.

Spadge paused and looked her straight in the eye.

'If it's any business of yourn.'

We shivered with pleasure at this defiance, Spadge leisurely made for the door.

'Sit down this instant!' Crabby suddenly screamed. 'I won't have it!'

'Ta-ta,' said Spadge.

Then Crabby sprang like a yellow cat, spitting and clawing with rage. She caught Spadge in the doorway and fell upon him. There was a shameful moment of heavy breathing and scuffling, while the teacher tore at his clothes. Spadge caught her hands in his great red fists and held her at arm's length, struggling.

'Come and help me, someone!' wailed Crabby, demented. But nobody moved; we just watched. We saw Spadge lift her up and place her on the top of the cupboard, then walk out of the door and away. There was a moment of silence, then we all laid down our pens and began to stamp on the floor in unison. Crabby stayed where she was, on top of the cupboard, drumming her heels and weeping.

Laurie Lee

WORD BANK

defiance deliberate disobedience

goading tormenting

inevitable unavoidable

in unison all together

lank long and straight

leer a nasty look

levitation rising and floating in the air

militant aggressive, warlike

natural manifestation of a person whose character was just like, a living version of

picking oakum picking old rope to pieces, an old-fashioned prison punishment

preceded coming or going before

pried peered in, was nosy

punitive wanting to punish

seldom rarely, not often

solar plexus nerves at the pit of the stomach

stocks medieval punishment device that kept the prisoner sitting

unintelligible impossible to understand

yourn your

Language questions

1 Look at these phrases and for each one decide on the verb tense.
Hint Ask yourself when it is happening.

- She crouched
- I will not have it
- We were surprised
- She appears in my recollection

- And where are you going?
- Crabby suddenly screamed
- We sat locked in our stocks
- Crabby sprang like a yellow cat

2 Look at this list of verbs. Fill in the grid for each one and then try to work out whether it is regular or irregular.
Hint Look at what happens to the verb in the past tense to see if it is regular or irregular.

Verb example	Infinitive	Present tense	Past tense	Regular or irregular?
crept	To creep	creep(s)	crept	irregular
knew	To know	know(s)	knew	irregular
stood				
said				
sprang				
knocked				
smelt				
came				
gave				
squeezed				
groaned				
tore				

Write a short explanation of how you could spot which verbs were regular or irregular.

3 Read this passage and correct all verb forms that are used incorrectly.

> According to the passage, Crabby seemed rather cruel. For example, she scared the pupils, springed on them and knowed that they might mess about. In the class, pupils sitted in silence but one day, Spadge Hopkins beginned to lose his patience with the teacher and catched her in his hands, lifting her up on to the cupboard. He leaved her there.

How did you know that some verbs needed changing?

4 Look at the paragraph below. The highlighted verbs are all irregular in the past tense.

> As the teacher spoke, the class felt nervous. She was the sort of woman who often threw board rubbers at the class and once she began ranting, there was usually no stopping her. She crept around the room and when she found the culprit, tore into them and told them off in the most humiliating way. She said that she had had enough.

The chart shows you how the highlighted verbs have changed from the present to the past tense by showing their endings.

Past tense (irregular)	Infinitive	Present ending	Past ending
spoke	To speak	eak(s)	oke
felt	To feel	eel(s)/ell(s)	elt
threw	To throw	ow(s)	ew
began	To begin	in(s)	an
crept	To creep	eep(s)	ept
found	To find	ind(s)	ound
tore	To tear	ear(s)	ore
told	To tell	ell(s)	old
said	To say	ay(s)	aid

Now read this passage that contains many irregular verbs.

The wind blew menacingly around the hills, dust swept in the playground and Crabby's temper wound up even more. Suddenly a window broke. The children knew that they would have to go home early. As they were leaving, one of the class ground pieces of the glass into the floor and a girl tripped and cut herself on it. The child wept and the jumper that she wore was ripped. Crabby dealt with the situation and kept the child under observation until her parents collected her. The wind outside grew worse and the glass in the windows rang violently. Crabby met the girl's parents outside the school and told them what had happened. Her father, being a glazier, said that she could have some glass for free as he had not paid for it anyway. When they had left, Crabby sat in the classroom and drank a calming cup of tea.

▶ Look at the present and past endings in columns 3 and 4 below. Find examples of verbs that follow these patterns in the passage that you have just read. Fill in the verbs you find in the passage and their infinitive (full form). An example is done for you.

Hint If there is more than one example, fill in all of them.

Past tense (irregular)	Infinitive	Present ending	Past ending
broke	To break	eak(s)	oke
		eal(s)	elt/ealt
		ow(s)	ew
		ing(s)/ink(s)	ang/ank
		eep(s)	ept
		ind(s)	ound
		ear(s)	ore
		ell(s)	old
		ay(s)	aid

Some of these verbs might have been difficult to place but you should now understand that tricky verbs can be easier to use if we remember these patterns.

Comprehension

 1   Describe what Crabby looks like. Give three points.

 2   What sort of things does Crabby do to make Laurie Lee call her 'a terror'?

 3   What is Crabby's catchphrase that pupils use to imitate her in the playground? Why do you think they imitate her?

 4   How does the writer describe Crabby's teaching? Select the most appropriate answer:
- ▶ a good teacher who taught the class a lot
- ▶ a teacher whose lessons were nothing special or worth remembering
- ▶ a monster who terrorized children.

5   Laurie Lee uses many exclamation marks when remembering Crabby's speech. What does this tell you about how she speaks to her pupils?

6   Laurie Lee says that he and his classmates would rather have been outside doing other things. He says of being in school 'we sat locked in our stocks'. What does this tell you about how he felt at school?

7   Fill in the chart below with details about Spadge Hopkins.

What Spadge looks like	How he behaves	How Crabby treats him

 8   Pick out the sentence which shows how the rest of the class enjoyed the sight of Spadge disobeying Crabby.

 9   Why do you think Laurie Lee remembers school life so clearly and vividly? Explain in a short paragraph.

Extended response

How does Laurie Lee present Crabby's character in the extract?

This question wants you to examine how the author reveals Crabby's character to the reader. The key points to look at are:

- ▶ how Laurie Lee describes Crabby
  Hint Look at the opening paragraph for a physical description of her (he compares her with an animal here).
- ▶ how Crabby speaks to the children
  Hint Look at the second and fourth paragraphs in particular (also look back at Comprehension question 5).
- ▶ how Crabby behaves
  Hint Look at how she treats Spadge and what Laurie Lee says about her in paragraphs six and seven.
- ▶ what the children think of her (especially Spadge Hopkins)
  Hint Look at how the children behave in the playground and how Spadge reacts to Crabby (also look back at the final Comprehension question).
- ▶ What effect do you think Crabby would have on the reader?
  Hint Think about what Laurie Lee wants us to understand about her and why he has written so clearly about her.

Be sure to use what you learnt in the Comprehension section to help you answer this question.

Speaking and listening

1 **Pairs**

What advice would you give to Crabby to improve her teaching and relationship with her pupils?

- ▶ Think about how she behaves towards them.
- ▶ Is this what you expect from your teacher?
- ▶ How does Crabby talk to the class? Does she need to work on her skills here?

▶ How would you explain to her how the pupils feel about her as a person?

Draw up a list of action points for Crabby to improve her teaching (be prepared to report these to the rest of the class and keep them for the next activity).

2 Pairs/Class

In pairs, one as Crabby and the other as a school inspector, devise the interview where the inspector gives Crabby feedback on her teaching and offers action points for future development. Use your notes from question one. Present the interview in role and think about how Crabby might react and speak – for example would she treat the inspector in the same way as the children?

Watch some other pairs and then as a class, discuss the different interpretations of Crabby's character that you have seen.
▶ Which Crabby was most like the one in the extract?
▶ Which one seemed really menacing and rude to the inspector?
▶ Which one seemed most different from the extract? Why?

TEXT B

This scene is from the comedy series *Blackadder*. In this, the final episode of the final series, Blackadder, Baldrick, and George are on the front line waiting for the big push and the end of the First World War. Melchett is their commander in the army, and Darling is his assistant. Earlier in the episode, Blackadder was pretending to be mad, hoping this would get him sent home.

Richard Curtis is a well-known comedy writer who has produced scripts for *The Vicar of Dibley*, *Four Weddings and a Funeral* and more recently *Notting Hill*. Ben Elton began his career as an actor and comedian but has gone on to write several books, have his own television show and write scripts for famous programmes such as the *Blackadder* series.

Blackadder Goes Forth

DARLING	Ten shun!

ALL STAND TO ATTENTION.

MELCHETT	At ease. Fine body of men out there.
BLACKADDER	Yes, sir – shortly to become fine bodies of men.
MELCHETT	Oh, nonsense. You'll pull through. I remember when we thrashed the old Harrovians back in 1895, they all said we'd never get through their back line – but we ducked and we bobbed and we wove and we damn well won the game, 15–4.
BLACKADDER	Yes, sir – but the Harrow full back wasn't armed with a heavy machine-gun.
MELCHETT	No, that's a good point. Make a note, Darling: recommendation for the Harrow governors, heavy machine-guns for full backs. Excellent idea, Blackadder. Now then, Private – looking forward to giving those Frenchies a good licking?
DARLING	No, sir, it's the Germans we'll be licking.
MELCHETT	Don't be revolting, Darling! I wouldn't lick a German if he was glazed in honey.
DARLING	Sorry, sir.
MELCHETT	Now you, soldier, do you love your country, soldier?
BALDRICK	Certainly do, sir.
MELCHETT	And do you love your king?
BALDRICK	Certainly don't, sir.
MELCHETT	Why not?
BALDRICK	My mum told me never to trust men with beards.
MELCHETT	Excellent native Cockney wit. (*He hits Baldrick*) Well, good luck to all of you. Sorry that I can't be with you, but… obviously there's no place in the front line for an old general with a dicky heart and a wooden bladder.

HE TURNS TO GO.

Oh, George, by the way, if you feel like coming back to HQ – hear the results as they come in tomorrow – there's a spare place in the car.

BLACKADDER LOOKS AT GEORGE.

GEORGE	Oh, no, thank you, sir. Wouldn't miss this for the world. I'm as excited as an excited person who's got a special reason to be excited.

MELCHETT	That's my boy! Must be going – tally-ho and pip pip all. I'll see you all in Berlin for coffee and cake.
	DARLING SPITS OUT COFFEE.
	What is the matter with you today, Darling? I'm terribly sorry, Blackadder. Come on, Darling – we're going.
	THEY EXIT. BLACKADDER SINKS IN DESPAIR.
GEORGE	By Jove, sir – I'm glad you're not barking any more.
BLACKADDER	Thank you, George – although it looks like you are. You were offered a way out and you didn't take it.
GEORGE	Absolutely not, sir, can't wait to get stuck into the Boche.
BLACKADDER	(*Exasperated*) You won't get time to get stuck into the Boche. We'll all be cut to pieces by machine-gun fire before we have time to yell 'Charge'.
GEORGE	So what shall we do now?
BALDRICK	Shall I do my war poem, sir?
BLACKADDER	How hurt will you be if I give the honest answer, which is, 'No – I'd rather French-kiss a skunk'?
BALDRICK	So would I, sir.
BLACKADDER	Good, fire away, Baldrick.
BALDRICK	*Hear the words I sing.* *War's a horrid thing.* *But still I sing, sing, sing* *Ding a ling a ling.*
GEORGE	(Clapping) Bravo!
BLACKADDER	It started badly, it tailed off a little in the middle and the less said about the end the better – but apart from that it was excellent.
BALDRICK	Shall I do another one then, sir?
BLACKADDER	We wouldn't want to exhaust you.
BALDRICK	Oh, don't worry, I could go on all night.
BLACKADDER	Not with a bayonet through the neck you couldn't.
BALDRICK	This one's called 'The German Guns'.
GEORGE	Oh, spiffing! Let's hear that!
	BLACKADDER PUTS HIS HEAD IN HIS HANDS.

BALDRICK	*Boom, boom, boom, boom,* *Boom, boom, boom* *Boom boom boom boom.*
BLACKADDER	*Boom boom boom?*
BALDRICK	How did you guess?
GEORGE	Gosh! Spooky, eh?
BLACKADDER	(*Wildly*) I'm sorry, but I've just got to get out of here.
BALDRICK	I have a cunning plan, sir.
BLACKADDER	All right, Baldrick, for old time's sake.
BALDRICK	You phone Field Marshall Haig and ask him to get you out of here.
BLACKADDER	Baldrick, even by your standards, it's pathetic. I've only ever met Field Marshall Haig once and it was over twenty years ago – and my God, you've got it, you've got it!
	HE KISSES BALDRICK.
BALDRICK	Well, if I've got it, you've got it too, now, sir.
BLACKADDER	I can't believe I've been so stupid! One phone call will do it – one phone call and I'll be free. Let's see – it's 3.30 – I'll call about quarter to six. Excellent, excellent! Ah! (Huge satisfied sigh) Now where were we? I must get packing.
GEORGE	You know I won't half miss you chaps after the war.
BALDRICK	Don't worry, Lieutenant, I'll come visit you.
GEORGE	Oh, will you really? Bravo, yes! Jump in the jalopy and come down to stay in the country. We can relive the old times.

Richard Curtis and *Ben Elton*

WORD BANK

Boche the Germans
by Jove an exclamation like 'my goodness'
exasperated at the end of his

tether, fed up
Frenchies the French
Harrovians students from the public school Harrow

HQ headquarters
jalopy an unreliable old car

Comparison

 1 Who does Melchett think the British are fighting against?

 2 What reasons does Melchett give for not being able to be on the front line?

 3 How does George show his stupidity when Melchett offers him a lift back to HQ?

4 Look at what Blackadder says about Baldrick's poem:

> It started badly, it tailed off a little in the middle and the less said about the end the better – but apart from that it was excellent.

Does Blackadder really mean this? Explain what you think.

5 You looked at the present and past tenses in Text A. This extract uses the future tense as well. We use the future tense to explain what is going to happen. Typical words that indicate the future tense are 'will', 'shall' and 'going to'.
Pick out four examples of the future tense from Text B other than those in the next question.

6 *Blackadder Goes Forth* is set in World War One. Many soldiers were killed as soon as they tried to advance towards the enemy. The audience watching *Blackadder* would know this.
Look at these lines spoken by characters in this scene:

> You'll pull through.
>
> I'll see you all in Berlin for coffee and cake.
>
> One phone call will do it – one phone call and I'll be free.
>
> Don't worry, Lieutenant, I'll come visit you.

What effect are these lines likely to have on the audience?

 7 The apostrophe can be used to contract verbs (e.g. 'I'm' for 'I am').
a) Find three examples of the future tense being contracted.
b) When do we tend to use contracted verbs the most?

Both writers create interesting and humorous characters. In Text A you looked at how Crabby is described and made to seem frightening to the children. In Text B you saw that George is simple and turns down the chance of avoiding death. We can tell several things about them from how they speak. For example, a character might:

▶ use old-fashioned and outdated language
▶ sound ridiculous and over-the-top
▶ add more sounds to a word, making it seem different
▶ repeat words for no reason.

a) Look at these things Crabby says in Text A:

> 1 'Good a-morning children'
>
> 2 'Ar Father…'
>
> 3 'A-smirking at that miserable Betty! I will not have it.'

Why do you think Laurie Lee lets us hear how Crabby speaks? Use the bullet points above to help you write a short answer.

b) Look at these extracts from George in Text B:

> 4 'I'm as excited as an excited person who's got a special reason to be excited.'
>
> 5 'By Jove, sir – I'm glad you're not barking any more.'
>
> 6 'Gosh!'
>
> 7 'You know I won't half miss you chaps after the war.'
>
> 8 'Oh will you really? Bravo, yes! Jump in the jalopy and come down to stay in the country. We can relive the old times.'

Why do you think the writers present George in this way? Use the bullet points above to help you write a short explanation.

c) Which character do you think is most amusing in how he/she speaks? Which one is the most ridiculous?
Write a short paragraph explaining your thoughts.

Writing assignments

1 Imagine that Baldrick explains his 'cunning plan' to Blackadder and that they escape death in World War One. Devise two scripted scenes between these two characters. The script will begin in the trenches (scene 1) but end elsewhere (scene 2).

In your writing try to:

▷ use a range of tenses to show the audience what has happened, what is happening and what is going to happen (look back at pages 33-35 for a reminder of tenses and how they are formed in some useful verbs)

▷ develop the characters of Blackadder (remember that he is really unpleasant to Baldrick) and Baldrick (don't forget that he is not too bright and often makes a fool of himself without realizing)

▷ devise a plan that will work – can you also make it funny?

▷ set your work out like the script in Text B with stage directions where appropriate, also making it clear where the scenes change

▷ keep the audience interested but don't make it obvious early on that the characters are going to survive the war.

2 Write Crabby's diary on the night of the Spadge Hopkins incident.

In your diary entry try to:

▷ use an informal style (you are not writing this for anyone to read – diaries are usually private)

▷ use a tone to match the character of Crabby (how does her mood seem most of the time?)

▷ write in the past tense on the whole (remember a diary is your thoughts on what has happened) – but you may use the future tense if Crabby is plotting what she will do to Spadge (remember the language focus on pages 33-35 can help you with tenses) think about how she would think, feel and what her opinion would be of Spadge Hopkins and the other children.

Drama
Chorus lines

In this unit you will:
- study an extract from a playscript adapted from a major Victorian novel
- focus on how and why a chorus is used in plays
- study a new playscript that uses a chorus
- write a scene of a playscript or design a storyboard.

Language focus

The Chorus

In a playscript, a chorus is a group of performers (ranging from one to many) who:
- narrate the story, often linking different scenes
- introduce new characters
- watch and comment on what is happening on stage
- speak directly to the audience
- interact with characters in the story and each other
- step into the action to take on specific roles
- speak alone and in unison to create 'special' effects.

TEXT A

Charles Dickens was born in Portsmouth in 1812. When he was 12, his father was sent to prison and Dickens had to leave school to work in a factory. He did return to school, but left at 15 to work as a reporter for the *Morning Chronicle*.

In 1833, Dickens began to write stories. These were first published as episodes in magazines and were enjoyed in the way that people enjoy soap operas today. He went on to write many novels using his own life experiences as material, as well as drawing attention to social injustices.

A Tale of Two Cities was published in weekly parts between April 30 and November 26 1859. The action is set in England and France at the time of the French Revolution – the two cities of the title are London and Paris.

This adaptation was written by Steve Barlow and Steve Skidmore. They have adapted a number of novels for the stage. They also write original drama scripts and are the authors of a growing number of humorous books for young people.

This extract from the playscript takes place some years before the famous storming of the Bastille prison on 14 July 1789. At this time, millions of ordinary people in France (like Gaspard) were condemned to a life of poverty, misery and starvation while aristocrats (like the Marquis) lived in luxury and demanded huge taxes from the poor. Pressure was growing to change such an unfair system. The time was ripe for revolution.

At the beginning, the Marquis, a ruthless, greedy nobleman, is down on his luck – he is short of money and unpopular at the French court. Annoyed by this turn of events, he leaves Paris for his estate in the country. The scene is set by a chorus of eight Citizens.

♛ A Tale of Two Cities ♛

ACT I

SCENE 2

The lights go up on the raised upstage area. The Marquis enters.
The Citizens enter and surround him. Downstage, in darkness the
Marquis' carriage is prepared, and his driver awaits him.

CITIZEN 7   Monseigneur is displeased.

CITIZEN 8   His wealth evaporates.

CITIZEN 7   He is frowned upon by the great men at court.

CITIZEN 8   He is low in fortune and out of favour.

CITIZEN 1   Monseigneur orders his carriage.   5

Lights up on the carriage. The Marquis descends and enters the carriage.
The Citizens follow him and take up a position downstage. The driver mounts.

We hear the rattle of the carriage as it starts and speeds up.
The lights on the carriage dim. Only the Citizens can be seen.

CITIZEN 2 He orders his driver to whip up the horses...

CITIZEN 3 ... and the man obeys.

CITIZEN 4 The carriage tears through the narrow streets...

CITIZEN 5 ... the crowded streets...

CITIZEN 6 ... where citizens scream and flee the mad charge of the   10
plunging horses and clattering carriage of monseigneur...

CITIZEN 1 ... until...

There is a break in the rhythm of the carriage. A scream rings out. It is
taken up by many voices. Enter a crowd, including Gaspard. A huddled
shape lies downstage. Gaspard howls and weeps over it. The lights come up.
The Marquis alights from the carriage. The Citizens rush to join the crowd.
Angry people reach for the driver who fends them off with his whip.

MARQUIS Driver! There was a jolt. What has gone wrong?

The crowd draws back. The frightened driver gestures with his whip.

CITIZEN 1 (*Humbly*) Pardon, Monsieur the Marquis, it is a child.

MARQUIS (*Indicating Gaspard*) Why does he make that abominable noise?   15
Is it his child?

CITIZEN 1 Excuse me, Monsieur the Marquis... it is a pity... yes.

Gaspard rises and appears to threaten the Marquis, who puts his
hand to his sword.

GASPARD Killed!

Gaspard throws himself on the body of the child and howls again.
The Marquis takes out his purse.

MARQUIS It is extraordinary to me that you people cannot take care of
yourselves and your children. One or the other of you is forever   20
in the way. How do I know what injury you have done my
horses? (*He throws a coin down*) Give him that.

The crowd mutters. Defarge enters. He goes to Gaspard. Mme Defarge
enters. She takes no part in the scene but sits aside and, composedly, knits.

DEFARGE   I know all, I know all. Be a brave man, my Gaspard. It is better for the poor little plaything to die so, than to live. It has died in a moment without pain. Could it have lived an hour as happily?   25

MARQUIS   You are a philosopher, you there. How do they call you?

DEFARGE   They call me Defarge.

MARQUIS   Of what trade?

DEFARGE   Monsieur the Marquis, vendor of wine.

MARQUIS   (*Throwing another coin*) Pick that up, philosopher and vendor   30 of wine, and spend it as you will. (*Turning*) The horses there, are they all right?

Defarge picks up the coin, spits on it, and throws it at the Marquis. He steps back and the crowd closes, hiding him from view.

MARQUIS   Who threw that?

There is no response. The crowd draws back. The Citizens return to their previous position downstage.

| MARQUIS | You dogs. I would ride my carriage over any of you very willingly, and exterminate you from the earth. | 35 |

The Marquis' gaze locks with Mme Defarge, who carries on knitting. The Marquis is discomfited. He turns and mounts his carriage.

| MARQUIS | Drive on! |

The lights fade except for tight spots on the Citizens.

CITIZEN 8	The Marquis drives on.
CITIZEN 7	He is satisfied...
CITIZEN 6	... as one who has accidentally broken some common thing...
CITIZEN 5	... and paid for it.	40
CITIZEN 4	He has outfaced the mob.
CITIZEN 3	Now, he arrives at his country estate...
CITIZEN 2	... at the village, poor and miserable, that lies in the very shadow of the great walls of his château.
CITIZEN 1	The people of the village are ragged.	45
CITIZEN 3	There are few children...
CITIZEN 4	... and no dogs.

The other Citizens look at Citizen 4 as if to ask 'why?'. Citizen 4 mimes eating. The Citizens nod glumly to indicate their understanding.

CITIZEN 5	Nobody is in the village square to welcome the Marquis home...
CITIZEN 6	... except the Marquis' servant, Gabelle...
CITIZEN 7	... a handful of starving peasants...	50
CITIZEN 5	... and a mender of roads.

Charles Dickens
*adapted by **Steve Barlow** and **Steve Skidmore***

WORD BANK

abominable offensive, awful
alights gets down
château a castle
a common thing something ordinary, nothing special
country estate land in the countryside, here including a castle and a village

discomfited baffled and uncomfortable
exterminate destroy; usually used to describe the killing of pests (like fleas) and vermin (like rats)
monseigneur a polite French form of address, meaning 'my lord'

Monsieur the Marquis a French aristocrat
philosopher a person who has a resigned attitude to events
vendor a person who sells something

Language questions

 1 Look at the opening (lines 1-5).
a) Who are the Citizens speaking about?
b) Who are the Citizens speaking to?
c) What do the Citizens say?
d) Why is this information important?

 2 Look at the next section (lines 6-12).
a) What are the Citizens doing here?
b) Why have they been given this role?

3 Look at lines 6-12 again.
Copy out the following sentences and fill in the gaps.
a) In describing the Marquis' journey through the streets of Paris, the Citizens use active verbs like _____, _____, _____ and _____ to create a vivid impression of speed, panic and danger.
b) The Citizens also use adjectives like _____, _____, _____, _____ and _____ to tell the audience more about the action and those involved in it. Adjectives help to paint a convincing visual picture.

 4 Think about the same lines again.
a) Why do you think such a short piece of dialogue is split between six Citizens?
b) What does this add to the atmosphere of this section of the playscript?

5   Now look at lines 38-41.
        What are the Citizens doing here?

6   Look at lines 14 and 17 where Citizen 1 steps into the action of the playscript.
        a) What kind of character does Citizen 1 become?
        b) How do you know?
           Hint Look closely at the language used and the stage directions.
        c) What does the way Citizen 1 speaks tell us about the Marquis – his position in society and his personality?

7   Find the point in the extract where the Citizens interact with each other.
        Hint Read the stage directions.
        a) What do they do?
        b) Why do they do this?

Comprehension

1   Which character is in a bad mood at the beginning of the extract?

2   What happens during the journey through the streets of Paris?

3   Name the father of the child.

4   What does Defarge do for a living?

5   Why are there no dogs in the village by the Marquis' château?

6   What is the Marquis' chief concern after the accident?
        Why is this shocking to us?

7   Why does the Marquis throw a coin for Gaspard?
        Hint There is a clue in the Citizens' lines on page 55.

8   Look at the Marquis' line:

> You dogs. I would ride my carriage over any of you very willingly, and exterminate you from the earth.

What does this line and particularly the word 'exterminate' tell you about the Marquis' opinion of ordinary people?

 What does the Marquis think of Defarge?
Think about:
▶ why he calls him a 'philosopher' – is this a compliment or an insult?
▶ why he throws him a coin – is this for the same reason as the one he gives to Gaspard?

 What does Defarge think of the Marquis?
(Hint) Think about Defarge's reaction to the coin thrown down by the Marquis.

Extended response

How do the authors show the character of the Marquis?

The question wants you to look at the different ways in which the Marquis' character is revealed to the audience. Use the headings and the bullet points below to help you structure your answer. Try to back up your opinions with evidence from the extract.

Factual information

What facts do the authors tell us about the Marquis?
▶ Who is he?
▶ What is his position in society?
▶ Where and how does he live?
How are these facts communicated – who tells us what?

Opinion

What do the following people in the extract think of the Marquis?
▶ the rich at court
▶ the poor living in Paris and on the Marquis' country estate
▶ the citizens

How do we know what their opinions are? Look closely at:

- the dialogue – what is said to and about the Marquis and how it is said (the tone of it)
- the actions – how they respond to the Marquis (look particularly at the way Citizen 1, Gaspard and Defarge behave towards him).

The Marquis' own behaviour

Does the Marquis' behaviour confirm the opinions of the other characters or does it offer us a different view of his character? Look carefully at:

- his words – what he says, how he says it and what this tells us about him
- his actions – what he does and how he treats people.

Conclusion

Sum up with your own view of the Marquis.

Speaking and listening

Group/class

Imagine that you are the police officer brought in to investigate the accident which caused the death of Gaspard's child. Your first task is to give a press conference to an invited audience of journalists. You will need to deliver a formal statement giving details about the accident. It is important to remember that, at this stage, no one has been found legally responsible for the accident.

Some tips for the police officer

When writing your statement:

- use standard English
- stick to the facts (you may have to make up a date, time and exact location for the accident)

- give the names of the people involved, but do not attach blame (again you may need to make up a name for Gaspard's child and the Marquis' driver)
- explain what your next move will be
- appeal for witnesses
- don't write more than 100 words.

Then go into role as the investigating officer and deliver your statement to a group of classmates in role as journalists. At the end of the statement, the 'journalists' will ask you questions. Think carefully about how you answer them. Stick to your brief and don't be tempted to blame anyone at this stage.

Some tips for the journalists

You have heard about the death of a child on the streets of Paris. You also know that there are lots of rumours flying around as to who was to blame for the accident. Your editor wants a powerful story for the front page of the newspaper. He/she is expecting you to ask the 'right' kind of questions to find out as much information as possible.

Before the press conference:

▶ work on your own or in pairs to prepare a list of questions to ask the investigating officer about the accident.

During the press conference:

▶ listen carefully to what the investigating officer says (and what he/she doesn't say) and make notes.

After the investigating officer's statement:

▶ ask the questions you have prepared and any others necessary to get a full picture of what happened

▶ don't be scared to ask 'difficult' questions. It's your job to get a 'good' story.

TEXT B

David Calcutt began his writing career as a poet. However, he found that his poems were getting longer and turning into mini-dramas and so he switched to writing plays. He has since written playscripts for radio, professional theatres, community groups, youth theatres, and schools.

The Labyrinth is a new play based on the story of Theseus, a heroic character from Greek myth. In this extract, Theseus is on his way to Athens to meet his father for the first time. He has decided to make the journey overland by the most dangerous route possible – a road haunted by thugs, criminals and monsters. The six members of the Athenian chorus take up the story.

The Labyrinth

ATHENIAN 2   He wanted to make a name for himself –

ATHENIAN 3   To become a hero like his hero, Heracles –

ATHENIAN 4   By ridding the road of all its roughnecks –

ATHENIAN 5   And there were plenty of them to be got rid of –

ATHENIAN 6   And the first one he came across was –   5

Athenian 1 takes on the role of Periphetes, taking up and wielding a large club.

PERIPHETES   Periphetes the Clubman!

Periphetes is a thug and speaks like one. This encounter, and the others that follow, are played with slapstick humour.

PERIPHETES   If anybody crosses my path, I take my club to them. Bash their skulls in! Spill their brains! And I'll serve you, stranger, like I've served all the others!

Periphetes swings the club wildly at Theseus, and Theseus dodges out of the way, as he narrates.

THESEUS   And he swung his club at me. And missed. Swung it again.   10
Missed again. I was too quick for him, too nimble on my feet.
Each time he swung, each time he missed. Until he began to
grow tired. He raised the club to swing again. I sidestepped,
grabbed the club, twisted it from his grip – (*He now has the
club*) – and broke his head with it!   15

Theseus hits Periphetes with the club. Periphetes falls, the other members of the Athenian chorus catch him and he re-joins them.

ATHENIAN 2   Then he continued with his journey –

ATHENIAN 3   One danger overcome, others awaiting.

ATHENIAN 4   And it wasn't long before he came upon the next –

ATHENIAN 5   At a place where two pine trees grew close to the road –

ATHENIAN 6   A man with a dagger and a wicked grin –   20

ATHENIAN I	A thoroughly nasty piece of work.

Athenian 2 takes on the role of Sinis, coming up behind Theseus and putting a dagger against his back. Sinis likes to cause pain. He thinks he's clever. He isn't.

SINIS	Sinis! That's my name. Hold it right there, stranger. Take your sword out of your belt. Nice and easy does it. No funny business. That's it. Drop it on the ground. Now step aside.

Theseus has dropped his sword and steps away from it, with Sinis behind him.

THESEUS	What do you intend to do with me? Run me through the ribs? Cut my throat?	25

SINIS	Oh, no! That's far too clean and simple. What I have in mind for you is something far more messy. Far more painful. Over there. Go on. Now, turn round and watch.

*Sinis pushes Theseus away. Theseus turns. Athenians 5 and 6 are
recruited by Sinis to stand as the two pine trees, and are bent over by
Sinis as Theseus narrates.*

THESEUS   Then he took hold of the two pine trees and bent them over   30
           until their tops touched the ground.

SINIS   They don't call me Sinis the Pinebender for nothing!

THESEUS   And he secured them there with two pegs. And I noticed that
           their branches were hung with bones, scraps of skin and hair,
           dried human flesh.   35

SINIS   Strange fruit these trees grow, eh? The fruits of my labours.
           And soon, my friend, you'll be growing there among them.

THESEUS   And there was a loop of rope attached to each treetop. And this
           villain gave me a particularly nasty grin, and said –

SINIS   Right. Put one of your hands in this loop, here, and the other   40
           hand in this loop here. Understand?

THESEUS   (*Acting stupid*) No. I'm sorry, I don't.

SINIS   What? It's simple enough. One hand here, the other hand
           here!

THESEUS   It's very complicated.   45

SINIS   No, it's not! It's easy. A child could do it. (*He grins nastily*)
           Several have, in fact.

THESEUS   (*Still pretending he doesn't get it*) Could you show me?

SINIS   All right. Watch.

           *Sinis 'attaches' a hand to one of the 'pine trees'. This is done simply by
           the Athenian playing the pine tree taking hold of one of Sinis' hands.*

SINIS   You put your hand into the loop of rope. Like this!   50

THESEUS   I think I'm beginning to get the idea. And I assume my other
           hand goes into the other loop. Something like this.

           Theseus attaches Sinis' other hand to the other 'pine tree'.

SINIS   That's it. You've got it now.

THESEUS	Then what?	
SINIS	Then comes the really nasty bit. I loose the pegs that are holding the trees down. Up they go! And up you go with them! One half that way. One half that way. And there you hang, ripped in two. Clever, eh? And nasty.	55
THESEUS	Very clever and very nasty. Like this, you mean?	
SINIS	Yes, like – !	60

Theseus frees the pine trees. They spring up. Sinis gives a loud scream and hangs suspended between them.

| THESEUS | And up he went. One half that way, one half that way. Ripped in two. And there he hung, and there he hangs, food for the ravens and crows. As he deserves. | |

Athenians 2, 5 and 6 rejoin the Athenian chorus. Theseus picks up his sword and puts it in his belt as he speaks.

| THESEUS | As for me, I picked up my sword, put it back in my belt, and continued with my journey. | 65 |

David Calcutt

WORD BANK

I'll serve you　I'll deal with you
nimble　able to move quickly

roughnecks　rough or violent
　people, thugs

wielding　holding and using

Comparison

1　Why does Theseus choose to travel by road to Athens?

2　a) Name Theseus' first attacker. How does Theseus defeat him?
　　b) Name Theseus' second attacker. How does Theseus deal with this opponent?

3　What is the role of the chorus in Text B?
　　Hint Look back at the information about the chorus on page 51.

Which other character tells the story in this extract?

 If you were directing this play, what would you want the remaining members of the chorus to do while Theseus was fighting with his attackers?

Choose either Theseus' fight with Periphetes or Sinis and write instructions in note form for the members of the chorus not directly involved in the action.

 Compare the tone of Texts A and B.

Remember: tone refers to the atmosphere of the extract (e.g. serious, light-hearted, tense, comic).

Write your answer as a short paragraph.

 Which role would you prefer – one of the Citizens in Text A or a member of the Athenian chorus in Text B? (You may specify which Citizen or Athenian, if you like.)

Explain your reasons in sentences.

8 Imagine a situation in which the same editor is working on *A Tale of Two Cities* and *The Labyrinth*. He or she doesn't want two playscripts with a chorus, but likes both stories. One chorus has to go!

Choose either *A Tale of Two Cities* or *The Labyrinth*.

Imagine that you are the playwright.

Write a list of reasons why it is essential that your chorus remains. You might also make some suggestions as to how the other playscript might work without a chorus.

Writing assignments

1 In Text B, Theseus defeated both Periphetes the Clubman and Sinis the Pinebender. However, he has still a long way to go before he reaches Athens, and more monstrous characters lie in wait for him.

Your task is to continue Theseus' journey to Athens in the same style as Text B and script the encounter between Theseus and his next opponent.

You don't need to stop at one. In the legend, Theseus defeats four more gruesome creatures before he reaches the safety of his father's court.

You will need to include the following:
▶ the six members of the Athenian chorus
▶ Theseus
▶ at least one 'monster' or 'villain'
▶ main stage directions and bracketed stage directions.

Look carefully at what the Athenians do and say (the Language focus on p51 will remind you of possible activities for a chorus). Look also at Theseus' role – he actually tells quite a lot of the story as well as speaking to his attackers.

You will also need to decide what kind of creature will do battle with Theseus. Build up a profile on your character to include:
▶ a good physical description
▶ a drawing, illustration or a photograph
▶ some details on its strengths, but also on its weaknesses
▶ what it plans to do to kill Theseus.

You can use your imagination to create your own 'monster' or you can research one of the many terrifying creatures from Greek myth or old legends. Alternatively, you could opt for a more up-to-date villain inspired by a book, a film or a computer game.

 2 Imagine that you are working on a TV or film adaptation of *A Tale of Two Cities*.
Your job is to storyboard the events of Text A from the Marquis' departure from Paris to his arrival at his country estate.

You must decide how many camera shots or frames you need and what each one will show. Here are some different kinds of shot you could use:

▷ close-up
▷ medium shot
▷ long shot
▷ high angle shot (looking down)
▷ low angle shot (looking up)
▷ zoom shot (the camera zooms in or out from the subject)
▷ pan shot (the camera moves across the scene, possibly to follow the action)
▷ tracking shot (the camera moves with the action)

Remember: each time you want a different camera shot (this could be a change of subject matter or a different kind of shot) you will need a new frame. Some frames will include dialogue and/or sound effects.

You could set out each frame like this:

Frame number

Location

Description of camera shot

Dialogue

Sound effects

You could also include sketches to demonstrate the camera shot if you find this useful. Put a sketch beside the description of the shot if you are including one.

2 Drama
Shakespeare's language

Aims

In this unit you will:
- study a famous speech written by William Shakespeare
- learn about Shakespeare's use of language and how it is different from the language we use today
- look at a fictional newspaper story based on Henry V's St Crispin's Day speech
- have a go at writing a speech, or designing advertising material, based on the extracts you have read.

Language focus

Shakespeare's verse

Shakespeare's plays are mainly written in what we call 'blank verse'. Here is an example of a complete sentence from Henry V, written in verse:

If we are marked to die, we are enough
To do our country loss, and if to live,
The fewer men, the greater share of honour.

You will see that:
- the sentence actually runs over three lines
- each new line starts with a capital letter
- the lines do not rhyme: this is why it is called 'blank' verse
- the lines are all about the same length.

Now look again at the first line:

If we are marked to die, we are enough

The first eight words of this line have one syllable (or beat) each, and the last word 'enough' has two syllables – making ten beats. Try to clap the rhythm of the line and say the words aloud at the same time:

If we are marked to die, we are enough
1 2 3   4   5 6 7 8 9 10

If we divide the ten beats into five lots of two, it looks like this:

If we/are marked/to die/we are/enough
1 2 / 3   4   / 5 6 / 7 8 / 9   10

Clap this rhythm again, but this time do a louder clap on beats 2, 4, 6, 8 and 10. When Shakespeare was writing in blank verse, he put more stress on the second, fourth, sixth, eighth and tenth syllables.

Iambic pentameter

A line with five 'pairs' of beats like this, and with the stress on every other beat, is called an iambic pentameter. This is the typical pattern used by Shakespeare in his plays. It influenced the words that Shakespeare chose and the order in which he put them down on paper.

One of the reasons Shakespeare may have used this rhythm is that it is a lot like ordinary speech. So when you read any of Shakespeare's text, try to think of it as speech and don't concentrate too hard on the rhythm. This will make it much easier to understand.

You may find some lines that don't seem to fit the pattern of five pairs of beats. Occasionally you may count eleven or twelve beats per line. This helps the verse sound more like real speech. Shakespeare may have meant it to work like this, or there might be other reasons, but critics are still debating it today.

Shakespeare's grammar

Shakespeare's sentences don't always use the same word order as modern sentences. People in sixteenth-century England did speak differently from how we do now, but Shakespeare also played with the word order in some sentences: for example, to make sure the right words were stressed. Look at this grid for examples of these features:

What we would say today	What Shakespeare would write
Why do you look so pale?	Why look you so pale?
Don't wish for a single man more.	Wish not one man more.
Evil things	Things evil
If men wear my garments	If men my garments wear
You	Thee / thou

'Thee'/'thou' was used in Shakespeare's time to show a close relationship or that you were talking to someone from a lower class. ('You'/'ye' was used among the aristocracy and in formal situations.)

Lost words

Shakespeare also used 'old' forms of words which are no longer used in standard English, though some of them can still be found in some regional dialects:

Shakespearean form	Standard English
hath, doth	has, does
Methinks	It seems to me
I pray thee Prithee	Please
Coz	Cousin
'Tis	It is

TEXT A

William Shakespeare was born at Stratford-upon-Avon in 1564. By 1592 he was earning money as an actor and a playwright. He is probably England's most famous writer and his plays are now performed on stage all over the world. Many (including *Henry V*) have been made into successful films.

Henry V was designed to stir patriotic feelings. It tells the story of a young king who led the English armies to a famous victory over the French at the Battle of Agincourt. The battle was actually won because of the English bowmen with their longbows, but Shakespeare's play ignores this and concentrated on Henry's role. Shakespeare presents him as a wise, brave, Christian king – and the hero of the story.

The following extract takes place on the eve of the battle. After initial success, the English army is now in a bad way. Many have died due to illness or battle injuries. The leaders of the French troops are confident of victory. The French soldiers are fresh and they far outnumber the English. What can Henry do?

STYLE NOTE: Kings were expected to speak in a grand style and Henry lives up to that expectation. Most of his speeches in the play – whether they are spoken to crowds or individuals – sound as if they ought to be addressed to a huge audience. They are designed to stir the blood of both the characters on stage and the people in the theatre.

(Because Henry's long speech is quite difficult , a modern adaptation has been given on the right-hand side of the next few pages.)

King Henry V

ACT 4, SCENE 3

Enter Gloucester, Bedford, Exeter, Erpingham with all his host, Salisbury and Westmorland.

GLOUCESTER   Where is the King?

BEDFORD   The King himself is rode to view their battle.

WESTMORLAND   Of fighting men they have full threescore thousand.

EXETER   There's five to one; besides, they all are fresh.

SALISBURY   God's arm strike with us! 'Tis a fearful odds.   5
God bye you, princes all: I'll to my charge.
If we no more meet till we meet in heaven,
Then joyfully, my noble lord of Bedford,
My dear lord Gloucester, and my good lord Exeter,
And my kind kinsman, warriors all, adieu.   10

BEDFORD   Farewell, good Salisbury, and good luck go with thee.

EXETER   Farewell, kind lord. Fight valiantly today.
And yet I do thee wrong to mind thee of it,
For thou art framed of the firm truth of valour.

[Exit Salisbury.]

BEDFORD   He is as full of valour as of kindness,   15
          Princely in both.

          Enter Henry.

WESTMORLAND   O that we now had here
          But one ten thousand of those men in England
          That do no work today!

HENRY   What's he that wishes so?
          My cousin Westmorland? No, my fair cousin:
          If we are marked to die, we are enough   20
          To do our country loss, and if to live,
          The fewer men, the greater share of honour.
          God's will, I pray thee wish not one man more.
          By Jove, I am not covetous for gold,
          Nor care I who doth feed upon my cost;   25
          It earns me not if men my garments wear:
          Such outward things dwell not in my desires.
          But if it be a sin to covet honour
          I am the most offending soul alive.
          No, faith, my coz, wish not a man from England.   30
          God's peace, I would not lose so great an honour
          As one man more, methinks, would share from me,
          For the best hope I have. O do not wish one more!
          Rather proclaim it, Westmorland, through my host,
          That he which hath no stomach to this fight,   35
          Let him depart; his passport shall be made
          And crowns for convoy put into his purse.
          We would not die in that man's company
          That fears his fellowship to die with us.
          This day is called the feast of Crispian.   40
          He that outlives this day and comes safe home
          Will stand a-tiptoe when this day is named
          And rouse him at the name of Crispian.
          He that shall see this day and live old age
          Will yearly on the vigil feast his neighbours,   45
          And say 'Tomorrow is Saint Crispian.'
          Then will he strip his sleeve and show his scars,
          And say 'These wounds I had on Crispin's day.'

WESTMORLAND   If only we had more men –
                One in ten thousand of those lying idle
                In England today.

HENRY   Who wishes that?
                You, cousin Westmorland? No.
                If we are doomed to die, we're enough
                For our country to mourn the loss. And if we live –
                Being so few – we'll get the greater share of glory.
                No, by God, don't wish one more man here!
                You know I'm not greedy for gold;
                I don't care how many feed at my expense.
                As for my fine clothes – let any wear them!
                I have no hunger for such outward shows of wealth.
                But greedy for glory I am!
                And if that's a sin, there's no greater sinner than I!
                Don't wish for a single man more from England, cousin.
                I wouldn't share a single part
                Of the honour and glory due to me, with one man more –
                Hope of my soul's salvation depends on it!
                Rather than wish more, cousin, tell our troops
                That if any man here has no heart for this fight,
                If any doesn't have the appetite, he's free to go;
                We ourselves will pay his passage home!
                We've no desire to die in fellow company of any man
                Who fears to die in ours.
                Today's the feast-day of Saint Crispian.
                He that survives this day and returns to home and safety,
                He'll stand tall and proud whenever he hears the name of Crispian.

                He that sees this day through and lives to his old age,
                Each year, when that feast-day's eve comes round
                He'll ask his friends and neighbours in, feed them well,
                and say 'Tomorrow is Saint Crispian's Day!'
                Then he'll roll up his sleeves and show his scars,
                And say to all: 'I got these fighting on Saint Crispian's Day!'

Old men forget; yet all shall be forgot
But he'll remember, with advantages,　　　　　　　　　50
What feats he did that day. Then shall our names,
Familiar in his mouth as household words,
Harry the King, Bedford and Exeter
Warwick and Talbot, Salisbury and Gloucester,
Be in their flowing cups freshly remembered.　　　　55
This story shall the good man teach his son,
And Crispin Crispian shall ne'er go by
From this day to the ending of the world
But we in it shall be remembered,
We few, we happy few, we band of brothers.　　　　60
For he today that sheds his blood with me
Shall be my brother; be he ne'er so vile,
This day shall gentle his condition.
And gentlemen in England now abed
Shall think themselves accursed they were not here,　65
And hold their manhoods cheap whiles any speaks
That fought with us upon Saint Crispin's day.

Enter Salisbury.

SALISBURY　　My sovereign lord, bestow yourself with speed.
The French are bravely in their battles set
And will with all expedience charge on us.　　　　70

HENRY　　All things are ready, if our minds be so.

WESTMORLAND　　Perish the man whose mind is backward now!

HENRY　　Thou dost not wish more help from England, coz?

WESTMORLAND　　God's will, my liege, would you and I alone,
Without more help, could fight this royal battle!　　75

KING　　Why, now thou hast unwished five thousand men,
Which likes me better than to wish us one.
You know your places. God be with you all!

William Shakespeare

Old men's memories go, and though he might forget all else,
He'll remember this day's daring deeds –
And add to them to make them even more! And our names too,
Names dear and close to him as his own heart and home –
Harry the king, Bedford and Exeter,
Warwick, Talbot, Salisbury and Gloucester –
They'll be recalled anew as he drinks deep.
And that good man will tell his son the tale,
And with each passing of the feast of Crispin Crispian,
From this day to the end of time,
We'll be remembered –
We few, we happy few, we band of brothers.

David Calcutt

WORD BANK

backward reluctant

be he ne'er so vile however low-born he is

bestow yourself get yourself ready, arm yourself

bravely in their battles set confidently ready to start the battle

charge division (the soldiers under his command)

expedience speed

faith indeed

Feast of Crispian a saint's day: October 25

for thou art framed in the firm truth of valour because everything about you is brave and honourable

gentle his condition make him more honourable and noble

God bye you God be with you

hold their manhood cheap be ashamed of being a coward

I do thee wrong to mind thee of it for 'mind' read 'remind'

kinsman relative (meaning Westmorland)

likes me pleases me

my liege my royal lord

there's five to one there are five times as many French soldiers as English

threescore thousand sixty thousand

to view their battle to look at the position of the French armies

vigil the evening before the feast-day

would ... if only, I wish

Language questions

Note: you must answer these questions by looking at Shakespeare's text, not at the modern version.

 Find at least one example of the following from the Shakespeare extract. Write down each example and the appropriate line reference.

- ▶ a sentence that runs over more than one line of verse
- ▶ a line of verse written in true iambic pentameter
- ▶ a line of verse, with 10 syllables, split between two characters
- ▶ a line of verse with more than 10 syllables
- ▶ a line of verse with less than 10 syllables (look between lines 1-10).

Compare your findings with other people in your class.

 Draw a table like the one below.

Word order in sentences	What Shakespeare writes	What we would write

Find at least five examples of Shakespeare's unfamiliar word order in Text A. Record these in the left-hand column. Then re-write the words in a more familiar order in the right-hand column.

 Make up three simple questions and write them down in the way that was common in Shakespeare's time.

Hint The first entry in the grid on page 69 will help you.

 When we want to tell someone to do something or give an order, we use a form of verb called an **imperative**. It usually comes first in the word order of a phrase or a sentence, e.g. '**Clear** the area, quickly'.

Henry issues a number of commands and uses verbs as imperatives. Look up the following line references:

- ▶ line 30
- ▶ line 34
- ▶ line 36

Write down Henry's command and underline the verb used as an imperative.

Choose the right definition – alliteration is:
- a Japanese poem
- a phrase where a number of words begin with the same letter or sound
- a comparison between two things using the words 'like' or 'as' when words sound the same but have different meanings.

Then find as many examples as you can of Henry's use of alliteration.

 Make a list of all the different forms of the future tense used by Henry in lines 40-60. Why do you think he chooses to talk about the future here, rather than the battle? Write a sentence giving your opinion.

Comprehension

Note: you may look at both versions of the text to answer these questions.

 Who is Henry speaking to in lines 18-39? What is this person's relationship to the king?

2 Look at lines 24-29. Two of the statements below are true. Copy out the correct ones.
- Henry is not greedy for gold.
- Henry gets angry if anyone wears his clothes.
- Henry is worried about the cost of food for his soldiers.
- Henry says his biggest sin is his desire for honour.
- Henry needs to earn some money for food and clothes.

3 How many times does Henry tell Westmorland not to wish for more men? Count the times and give a line reference for each.

 a) What does Henry offer any soldier who 'hath no stomach to this fight'?
b) What is his opinion of such men? Find a quotation from the passage to support your answer.

5 According to Henry, what will the survivors of the battle do each year on the eve of St Crispin's Day?

6 Which of the following words and phrases would you use to describe Henry?

> ▶ weak   ▶ scared
> ▶ brave   ▶ strong leader
> ▶ loves honour

Can you add to the list?

Find an example of something which Henry says or does in Text A to support each of your chosen words. You could set it out like this:

> We know Henry is a strong leader because he...

7 Look at lines 61-67. Using what you have learned about Shakespeare's language and grammar, try to write these lines in simple modern English.

Before you start, think about the following things:

▶ How many sentences are there in these six lines of verse?

▶ Pick out the strange word orders and try to reorganize them.

▶ Translate difficult words into familiar modern English (the Word bank should help you).

Extended response

How does Henry inspire his tired soldiers before the battle of Agincourt?

The question wants you to look at what Henry says (the arguments he uses) to rally his troops and get them in fighting mood; and how he says it (the techniques he uses). (Remember, the English soldiers are exhausted and demoralized; they know the French army outnumbers them five to one and they stand little chance of surviving, let alone winning.)

Use the bullet points below to structure your answer. Write a short paragraph for each.

▶ What is the first thing that Henry tells his soldiers (lines 24-39)? Look carefully at his choice of words. What effect do you think this would have on his men?

▶ Look at lines 40-62. How does Henry create a feeling of team spirit in these lines? (Look at how he uses St Crispin's Day; the names of his lords; the words 'brother' and 'brothers'.)

▶ What kind of vision of the future does Henry create for the men who fought at Agincourt? How does he do this? (Look at the verb tenses and his choice of vocabulary.) What does he leave out?

▶ How does Henry reinforce his message? Look closely at the language of his speech – the repetition of words; the use of alliteration; imperatives or commands.

▶ Finally, look at the closing lines of Henry's speech (lines 61-67). Is this a good way to finish? How do you think the soldiers will feel at the end of the speech?

Speaking and listening

Individual

Imagine that you are a war correspondent reporting on the events in the English camp before Agincourt. Your job is to send back a report lasting no more than 1-2 minutes (when read aloud) on the mood in the English camp before the battle.

Your report must cover:

▶ how the soldiers feel (see the introduction to Text A, on page 70, for clues)

▶ some information about the French forces (see lines 3-4)

▶ Henry's speech (see lines 18-67)

▶ reactions to this speech (you will need to imagine these).

Write and then perform your report for a TV or radio news bulletin.

Remember: your report will be heard by a wide audience. Keep the tone formal, speak slowly and clearly and use standard English. You could record this on audio or video tape.

WORD BANK

aftermath after-effects
conscription compulsory military service
jubilant overjoyed

TEXT B

This fictional newspaper story comes from *The Bard – The Tabloid Shakespeare* by Nick Page. The author has taken scenes and speeches from Shakespeare's plays and reworked them as pieces of 'joke' tabloid journalism. His intention is to amuse his audience. This particular spoof story was inspired by Henry 's speech from Text A.

THE BARD   *Every Crispin Day*   *80*

FRENCH FRIED CRISP'N' DIE

Crispin Day Massacre Of French Forces

'We're Like One Big Happy Family,' Says King

'We few, we happy few, we band of brothers, we three kings, we are the champions!'

Those were the words of a jubilant King Henry in the aftermath of an astonishing victory at Agincourt. The English army beat the French who outnumbered them five to one.

'It's a victory for our superior courage, superior nerve and superior strength,' said one commander. 'That plus the fact we have these flipping great longbows and they don't.'

Jubilant

The King was in jubilant mood.
'We lost hardly any men,' he said. 'Just Edward Duke of York, Earl of Suffolk, Sir Richard Keighley, Davy Gam and a few other commoners that nobody bothers much about.'

Now the King is intent on securing a lasting peace with France and possibly getting his hands on the daughter of the King.

'They have offered me the hand of their daughter in marriage,' said the King, 'with the rest of her phased in by 1420.'

Bring Back Work For Welfare

'Give Us Ten Thousand More' Says Duke

On the eve of the battle a leading nobleman called for national conscription of all the unemployed.

'If we had but one ten thousand of all those in England who do no work today!' exclaimed the Duke of Westmorland. 'Then we'd have... er... ten thousand more men than we do at the moment. And that's a fact.'

The King, however, has dismissed the scheme.
'Apart from the obvious fact that we are due to fight in a few hours' time and they're still in their beds, I believe that the fewer men the greater share of honour.'

Comparison

 1　This 'tabloid story' uses a common headline technique – a play on words (or pun) based on the subject of the story. Write a few sentences explaining the play on words in the main headline – 'French Fried Crisp'n' Dic' – and why this is amusing, but also in rather bad taste.

Hint 'Crisp 'n' Dry' is an oil used for cooking chips.

 2　Where would you hear or read the following:
- ▶ 'we three kings'
- ▶ 'we are the champions'?

Why do you think the author used them?

What is your response to these as a reader?

 3　Read the last paragraph of the main article. Explain the play on words there.

 4　Look at what the king says under the heading 'Jubilant'. How is he different from Henry in the play? Think about:
- ▶ the way he presents the English losses
- ▶ his attitude to lower-class soldiers.

Hint Compare this with lines 61–67 in Text A and your answer to Comprehension question 8.

 5　Compare the text of both news articles with Text A. Which words, phrases and information are taken directly from Text A? You could record your findings on a grid.

6　What is your opinion of these 'spoof' news stories?

Did you find them amusing? If so, explain why.

Is there anything about them you didn't like? If so, explain why.

Writing assignments

For both of these activities, the Language focus on persuasive style, on page 20, may help you.

1 A school sports team has to play an important match to stay in a special competition. The honour of the school depends on their success and everyone wants them to win – in spite of the fact that they are the underdogs. The team is despondent; they are all tired, and some of them are injured – perhaps the star player can't make the match.

At a crucial moment in the action, the team captain must rally the team with a speech designed to inspire their fighting spirit and spur them on to victory.

Write the team captain's speech. It may help to jot down some notes and ideas under the following headings:

Main characters
- personalities
- relationships between team members
- personal problems that may affect a team member's performance

Where the scene takes place
- in the changing rooms
- on a team bus
- at someone's house

Before you write the speech think about:
▶ a short build-up to it through dialogue or stage directions
▶ what the captain will say to rally the team
▶ how each character will react – will you show this through speech or stage directions?
▶ what instruction you will give on how your characters speak their lines (Shakespeare does not offer much help here, but more modern playwrights usually do in the form of bracketed stage directions, as in the texts in Drama Unit 1).

2 Imagine that you have been employed to produce advertising material to encourage more men to join Henry V's army. You can decide how you will reach your chosen audience. Here are some suggestions:

▶ recruitment poster
▶ brochure
▶ leaflet
▶ website
▶ magazine or TV advertisement.

What will your message be? Will you tempt your target audience with a promise of a life of honour and glory; or will you appeal to their sense of duty and guilt by making them feel less than 'real' men if they don't join up?

Your text could include direct quotations from Henry's speech and you could use visual images of the king and his followers.

Before you start, you could research some of the current recruitment material produced by the armed forces. You should be able to find printed material from recruitment offices and information on the Internet. You may also have seen TV advertisements.

You could also research posters designed to recruit soldiers for past wars. Michael Foreman's *War Game* contains an interesting selection of examples from the First World War. You will find other material in history books and on the Internet.

1 Fiction
The final frontier

Aims

In this unit you will:
- explore some features of science fiction writing
- look at ways that writers build tension in stories
- compare fiction and non-fiction texts about alien creatures
- practise building tension in your own narrative writing.

Language focus

Tension makes us want to keep reading, to find out what happens next. Writers and film-makers use different techniques to build tension. In this unit, we will be looking at three main ways writers might increase tension in a piece.

What will happen?

Writers can build expectation about what **might** happen next:

> I looked into the woods and wondered what was in there.

or

> I looked into the woods and thought something was moving around.

As readers, we want to know what might be in the woods, so we read on.

When will it happen?

Once we are expecting something to happen, the writer can make the situation more tense by **keeping us waiting** for the next event.

If you watch a scary TV programme, sometimes you know something frightening is going to happen, but there is a conversation or some minor action to delay it. The pause builds tension because we know something is going to happen – but not when.

In a story, the writer might suddenly switch from action to description, so that the pace of the story decreases, keeping us waiting to get back to the action.

Using words that create tension and drama

Emotive vocabulary can create tension. These are words that trigger an emotional response in us – for example, words like 'danger', 'darkness', 'fear', 'hope'.

Writers can also use phrasing which creates a feeling of drama:

> He could feel the fear rising through his body: something – he didn't know what – was moving closer.

This combines emotive words like 'fear' with dramatic phrasing: 'fear rising', 'moving closer'. Notice how much more dramatic the phrases are than: 'he felt scared – something was approaching'.

Science fiction

Science fiction explores technology and the future. The best stories have real tension about what might happen next; and stories set in space have a lot of scope for drama.

One feature of science fiction is the amount of technical language it can include. Writers may use a lot of technical terms to give an impression of advanced technology and to make the stories they are writing seem more believable. Often it is not necessary to understand all the technical terms in order to follow the story; they can be there to provide an atmosphere. Here is an example:

> Velocity 22.4c. Operating-temperature: normal. Ship-temperature: 37°C. Air pressure: 778mm.

These technical terms help to create the world of a spaceship, emphasizing that it is a technical environment. We don't need to understand the exact terms in order to see what kind of place the writer is creating.

TEXT A

James Blish was born in 1921, and started his writing career producing novelizations of *Star Trek* episodes. Later he wrote his own stories, many of them about outer space. They were often concerned with major themes, such as the future of science and religion.

Like a lot of science fiction writing, this story makes heavy use of technical terms to help create a feeling of high-tech science.

Common Time

Don't move.

It was the first thought that came into Garrard's mind when he awoke, and perhaps it saved his life. He lay where he was, strapped against the padding, listening to the round hum of the engines. That in itself was wrong; he should be unable to hear the overdrive at all.

He thought to himself: *Has it begun already?*

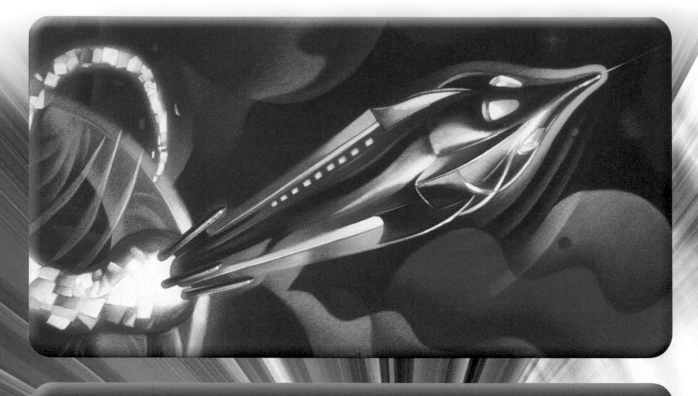

Otherwise everything seemed normal. The DFC-3 had crossed over into interstellar velocity, and he was still alive, and the ship was still functioning. The ship should at this moment be travelling at 22.4 times the speed of light – a neat 4,157,000 miles per second.

Somehow Garrard did not doubt that it was. On both previous tries, the ships had whiffed away towards Alpha Centauri at the proper moment when the overdrive should have cut in; and the split-second of residual image after they had vanished, subjected to spectroscopy, showed a Doppler shift which tallied with the acceleration predicted for that moment by Haertel.

The trouble was not that Brown and Cellini hadn't gotten away in good order. It was simply that neither of them had ever been heard from again.

Very slowly, he opened his eyes. His eyelids felt terrifically heavy. As far as he could judge from the pressure of the couch against his skin, the gravity was normal; nevertheless, moving his eyelids seemed almost an impossible job.

After long concentration, he got them fully open. The instrument-chassis was directly before him, extended over his diaphragm on its elbow-joint. Still without moving anything but his eyes – and those only with the utmost patience - he checked each of the meters. Velocity: 22.4 c. Operating-temperature: normal. Ship-temperature: 37°C. Air-pressure: 778 mm. Fuel: No. 1 tank full, No. 2 tank full, No. 3 tank full, No. 4 tank nine-tenths full. Gravity: 1 g. Calendar: stopped.

He looked at it closely, though his eyes seemed to focus very slowly, too. It was, of course, something more than a calendar – it was an all-purpose clock designed to show him the passage of seconds, as well as of the ten months his trip was supposed to take to the double star. But there was no doubt about it: the second-hand was motionless.

That was the second abnormality. Garrard felt an impulse to get up and see if he could start the clock again. Perhaps the trouble had been temporary and safely in the past. Immediately there sounded in his head the injunction he had drilled into himself for a full month before the trip had begun –

Don't move!

James Blish

WORD BANK

Alpha Centauri the nearest bright star to Earth's solar system

diaphragm a muscle under the ribs

Doppler shift a change in the colour something seems to be, that shows how fast it is moving

functioning working

injunction an order, warning

instrument-chassis a frame which holds dials, like the panel in front of a car's driver

interstellar velocity a speed fast enough to travel between stars

overdrive a kind of engine

residual image image left in space by something moving very fast

subjected to spectroscopy analysed with equipment that measures the radiation something gives off

tallied with matched

velocity speed

whiffed away whizzed away

Language questions

 Look at the first two words: *Don't move.*

a) Why do you think the writer places these on their own in a separate paragraph?

b) Why do you think they are in italics?

c) What effect does this opening of the story have upon the reader? Does it confuse us, interest us, make us want to read on?

 The next sentence helps the reader to make sense of the first two words. We learn that they are a character's thoughts. But look at the second part of the sentence: *and perhaps it saved his life.* Which word best describes this?

dramatic   surprising   interesting   descriptive   emotional

Now try to explain why you have chosen that word.

 Science fiction writers sometimes build tension by hinting that things are not working properly or not going according to plan. Here, Garrard hears something he shouldn't and thinks: *Has it begun already?*. Look at the use of the pronoun 'it' here. Usually we expect pronouns to refer back to a noun used earlier. But here it is not at all clear what 'it' might be referring to.

Try to explain the effect of using a pronoun in this way: how does it help to increase the tension?

4 Now think about words and phrases being used to build tension in the story. Which of the list below are most dramatic and most emotive? Look at the list and place the phrases on the scale of most to least dramatic.

most dramatic (builds tension) ____5 ____4 ____3 ____2 ____1 **least dramatic** (neutral)

a) perhaps it saved his life

b) everything seemed normal

c) neither of them had ever been heard of again

d) moving his eyelids seemed almost an impossible job

e) But there was no doubt about it: the second hand was motionless

Now choose one example from question 4 and try to say what it is that makes it dramatic. Think about:

- ▶ the way it hints at trouble
- ▶ the rhythm of the phrase
- ▶ the associations of the words
- ▶ the punctuation of the phrase.

6 We usually expect science fiction texts to use language that suggests scientific accuracy and high technology. This story uses a number of statistics and exact measurements:

> 22.4 times the speed of light
> a neat 4,157,000 miles per second
> velocity: 22.4 c

... and so on.

Play around with these scientific references. What is the effect if you change them from exact measurements to more generalized references? For example, add adverbial phrases like:

> Very quickly
> Quite slowly
> Fairly hot

How does the text begin to feel different? Does it stop feeling like science fiction?

Comprehension

1 What do you think the DFC-3 is?

2 What is Garrard's job?

3 Science fiction writers often build tension by hinting at things that have gone wrong, or that are not running as expected. Find three examples where there seem to be problems.

 We follow the story of Garrard in this text without being told much about him. For example, we do not learn what he looks like. By the end of the extract, what impression of his character have you gained? Write down three words which you think sum up what he is like.

 Read paragraph 5 again, and try not to get bogged down in the technical language. What does this paragraph tells us about the previous missions?

(Hint) Most of the information is near the beginning of the second sentence.

 The extract deliberately tells us little about Brown and Cellini.
a) Can you work out:
  ▶ who they were?
  ▶ what they did?
  ▶ why this led to Garrard's current mission?

b) Why do you think the writer only hints at their stories now? Does it affect the tension of Garrard's situation?

7 Write down a prediction about what you think will happen next in the story. See if you can back up your answer with something from the extract.

Extended response

How successfully does the writer build tension in the story?

Look back through your answers to the Language questions and the Comprehension section. They will help you to construct your answer. Try to comment on:
  ▶ the opening paragraph: how the writer gains the reader's attention
  ▶ how he hints at things going wrong to keep us reading
  ▶ how he uses dramatic language to hold our interest
  ▶ which parts of the story you find especially successful, and why
  ▶ which parts of the story you find least successful, and why.

TEXT B

Humans are fascinated by the thought of aliens. Many science fiction films, programmes and books are based on this idea. We are also obsessed with apparently true-life sightings of UFOs – unidentified flying objects. Read this factual account of some sightings which are supposed to have happened over Washington DC, USA, in the early 1950s...

The UFO Phenomenon

The spectacular began in the dying hours of July 19, 1952, when two radars picked up eight unidentified objects on their screens at Washington National Airport. Whatever the objects were, they were roaming the Washington area at speeds of between 100 and 130 miles per hour. They would suddenly accelerate to 'fantastically high speeds,' and leave the area. The long-range radar in Washington has a 100-mile radius, and was used for controlling all aircraft approaching the airport. The National Airport's control tower was equipped with a shorter range radar designed for handling planes in its immediate vicinity. Just east of the airport was Bolling Air Force Base, and ten miles futher east was Andrews Air Force Base, which were also equipped with short-range radar. All these airfields were linked by an intercom system. All three radars picked up the same unknown targets. One object was logged at 7000 miles per hour as it streaked across the screens, and it was not long before the UFOs were over the White House and the Capitol, both prohibited flying areas. Radar experts were called in to check the equipment, though it was clear that the odds against three radar-scopes developing identical faults were exceptionally high. They were found to be in good working order. Visual sightings were made as airline pilots came into the area and saw lights they could not identify. The lights were exactly where the radars were picking up UFOs.

A commercial airline pilot was talking to the control tower when he saw one of the lights. 'There's one – off to the right – and there it goes,' he said. As he reported, the controller had been watching the long-range radar. A UFO that had shown to the airliner's right disappeared from the scope at the very moment the pilot said it had.

One of the best ground sightings that night came when the long-range radar operator at the airport informed Andrews Air Force Base tower that a UFO was just south of them, directly over the Andrews radio station. When the tower operators looked out they saw a 'huge fiery orange sphere' hovering in the sky at exactly that position.

Incredible as it may see, no one thought to inform ATIC, and it was nearly daylight when a jet interceptor arrived over the area to investigate the phenomena. Its crew searched the skies, found nothing unusual, and left – but the UFOs had left the radar screens by then in any case.

A week later almost to the hour, the flying saucers were back over Washington to give a repeat performance. The same radar operators picked up several slow-moving targets at about 10:30 p.m. on July 26. The long-range radar operators began plotting them immediately. They alerted the control tower and Andrews Base, but it already had them on its screens and were plotting them. A call went out for jet interceptors. Once again there was a delay but two jets finally arrived soon after midnight. The UFOs mysteriously vanished from the screens just as the jets arrived. The pilots could see nothing during their search, and returned to base. Minutes after the jets left the Washington area the UFOs came back! The jets were called back, and this time when they reached the area, the UFOs remained. The controllers guided the pilots toward groups of targets, but each time the objects flew away at great speed before the pilots could see more than a strange light. At times it seemed that the lights were somehow monitoring the control tower conversations with the pilots, and responding before an aircraft had time to change course. On one occasion a light remained stationary as the jet pilot flew at it with full power. As he closed in the light suddenly disappeared, like a light being switched off. Both Washington sightings lasted several hours, and the second one gave some of the Air Force's top saucer experts an opportunity to rush to the airport, watch the radar screens, and listen to the pilots' accounts.

WORD BANK

airliner a large passenger aircraft
ATIC the Air Technical Intelligence Service
Capitol an important government building
commercial airline pilot pilot of a plane flying for business

dying hours last hours
immediate vicinity the area directly around something
jet interceptor a fast plane used to chase and stop other planes
monitoring listening in on
phenomena strange happenings

prohibited forbidden
radar equipment for tracking moving objects
scope a screen
spectacular an impressive display

Comparison

 1 Read the first paragraph. What are the unidentified objects doing that makes them seem different from aircraft?

 2 Why do you think experts were called in to check the radar equipment?

 3 What evidence is there that the strange sightings in the sky may have been UFOs? Try to find at least three clues.

 4 What makes this seem more like an extract from a non-fiction text, rather than a made-up story like Text A? Think about:

- ▶ the narrative voice: does it use 'I'/'we' or 'he'/'they'?
- ▶ use of dialogue
- ▶ reference to specific people and places
- ▶ whether the text uses emotive vocabulary to build tension.

Write your response using subheadings, like this:

> **Narrative voice**
> Text B is similar / dissimilar to Text A because...
>
> **Use of dialogue**
> Text B is similar / dissimilar to Text A because...

 5 Although Text B is non-fiction, does that mean that the writer does not build a feeling of tension? Look for the features you found in Text A. You could then discuss your findings with a partner.

Speaking and listening

Pairs/group

In pairs or a small group, discuss these questions about Text B:

- ▶ Does the extract answer all your questions about the UFOs?
- ▶ What questions does it leave you asking about the sightings of the mysterious lights?
- ▶ What theories can you think of to explain the strange lights?

> Are there any hints that we are not being given the whole story?
>
> Is there anything you find suspicious or disturbing in the report?

Discuss the questions, and then be prepared to share your responses with the rest of the class.

Writing assignments

1 Imagine that people on Earth are following Garrard's journey through space via the internet. The problems on the ship are suddenly reported in a newsflash on various websites. What would the newsflash say?

Write a 150-word report telling people that there seem to be problems. You might structure it like this:
- headline (e.g. 'Time problems hit space explorer')
- an account of what Garrard is doing – why he is on this mission
- what happened in the past
- what the technical problems seem to be

Keep your report factual, clear and informative. If you have already done Non-fiction and media unit 1, look back at the Language focus on pages 6-7 for hints on how to organize the story and how to make it dramatic, like a newspaper report.

2 Take Text B and make it into a story. Imagine someone is in Washington when the strange lights appear. How does he or she react? Does he or she telephone the police, or a friend? What happens next?

- Think about who your character is.
- Decide whether to use the first person ('I...') or third person ('She/he...')

Then begin writing your story. Think about how you will create drama and tension – the Language focus on pages 84–85 should help.

Fiction
Stories through diaries

Aims

In this unit you will:
- explore the genre of stories told through diaries
- explore features of formal and informal English
- learn about the concept of register
- compare two stories from different centuries
- compare the narrators' voices in the two texts.

Language focus

There are three different types of sentence. Writers use these different sentence types to create different effects, and to vary the pace of their writing.

1 Simple sentences, e.g.:

I saw the ship.

This contains one subject ('I') doing one action ('saw the ship'). The style is usually simple, straightforward and clear.

2 Compound sentences, e.g.:

I saw the ship and I ran down the beach but it was too late.

Each clause is listed one after another, and has the same weight and importance as the others; for that reason we say that the clauses are co-ordinated. The clauses are joined by the conjuctions 'and', 'but', and 'or'.

3 Complex sentences.
These are made of a main clause and a clause offering background information: a **subordinate** clause. They can come in several forms:

Example A   Once I saw the ship, I ran down the beach.

The main clause in Example A – the main message of the sentence – is 'I ran down the beach'; 'Once I saw the ship' is the subordinate clause, giving background information.

Example B Although I ran down the beach as soon as I saw the ship, I was too late.

'Although I ran down the beach as soon as I saw the ship' is the subordinate clause. 'I was too late' is the main clause.

Most writers use a variety of sentence styles. If they used the same style all the time, their story could become repetitive and boring. But this will depend on their audience: for example, stories for children will usually contain more simple and coordinated sentences, and fewer complex sentences.

Formal and informal styles in stories

Stories can be told in formal or informal styles, depending on what sort of feel the writer is aiming for.

	Features of a informal style	Features of a formal style
Text-level features	Like spoken language – not heavily structured. Sometimes disjointed. One idea doesn't always follow on logically from another, and there may be fewer discourse markers ('meanwhile... then... later'). The text may be more confusing at first because the sequence of events is less clear. A personal tone.	Often structured into sentences and paragraphs. Uses discourse markers to guide the reader from one idea to the next ('once upon a time... then... later').
Sentence-level features	Lots of compound (co-ordinated) sentences (in which clauses are linked by linked by 'and', 'but' and 'or'), giving a feel of spontaneous communication.	Formal sentence styles tend to use complex sentences (sentences including subordinate clauses), giving a feel of preparation and planning.
Word-level features	Usually less complex, more straightforward vocabulary.	Possibly more complex, precise vocabulary.

	Informal styles often use familiar, everyday words: often words taken from Old English – e.g. 'house' – rather than words taken from Latin – e.g. 'habitation'.	Formal styles often use words taken originally from Latin, e.g. 'congestion' rather than 'jam', 'estrangement' rather than 'split', 'provisions' rather than 'food'.

Stories in diary form

We can tell stories in many ways. Some are third person narratives (she/he/they) using the past tense – for example:

> Once upon a time there were three bears...

Others can use the styles of other genres, such as diaries, which use the first person voice ('I'):

> *March 11th*
> I set off early on my walk through the forest and wandered towards a house I hadn't seen before...

Diaries allow us to see inside a character's mind, to know what he or she is thinking. The style can often help us to get to know the character – for example, an informal, colloquial tone (as above) rather than a formal, complex one.

TEXT A

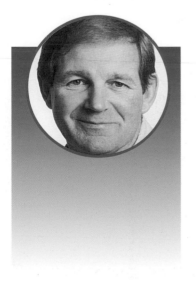

M ichael Morpurgo lives in the West Country where he writes and runs a small farm. He is well-known for his books for children, including *Why the Whales Came*, *The Ghost of Grania O'Malley* and *Waiting for Anya*.

The Wreck of the Zanzibar is set on the Scilly Isles, off the southern coast of Britain. It is 1907 and Laura lives on the islands with her family. She spends much of her time exploring the local beaches. Recent bad weather means that there is a shortage of food. In this extract, Laura is exploring a beach after a fierce storm...

The Wreck of the Zanzibar

September 8th

Today I found a turtle. I think it's called a leatherback turtle. I found one once before, but it was dead. This one has been washed up alive.

Father had sent me down to collect driftwood on Rushy Bay. He said there'd be plenty about after a storm like that. He was right.

I'd been there for half an hour or so heaping up the wood, before I noticed the turtle in the tideline of piled seaweed. I thought at first he was just a washed-up tree stump covered in seaweed.

He was upside down on the sand. I pulled the seaweed off him. His eyes were open, unblinking. He was more dead than alive, I thought. His flippers were quite still, and held out to the clouds above as if he was worshipping them. He was massive, as long as this bed, and wider. He had a face like a two hundred year old man, wizened and wrinkled and wise with a gently-smiling mouth.

I looked around, and there were more gulls gathering. They were silent, watching, waiting; and I knew well enough what they were waiting for. I pulled away more of the seaweed and saw that the gulls had been at him already. There was blood under his neck where the skin had been pecked. I had got there just in time. I bombarded the gulls with pebbles and they flew off protesting noisily, leaving me alone with my turtle.

I knew it would be impossible to roll him over, but I tried anyway. I could rock him back and forth on his shell, but I could not turn him over, no matter how hard I tried. After a while I gave up and sat down beside him on the sand. His eyes kept closing slowly as if he was dropping off to sleep, or maybe he was dying – I couldn't be sure. I stroked him under his chin where I thought he would like it, keeping my hand well away from his mouth.

A great curling stormwave broke and came tumbling towards us. When it went hissing back over the sand, it left behind a broken spar. It was as if the sea was telling me what to do. I dragged the spar up the beach. The I saw the turtle's head go back and his eyes closed. I've often seen seabirds like that. Once their heads go back there's nothing you can do. But I couldn't just let him die. I couldn't. I shouted at him. I shook him. I told him he wasn't to die, that I'd turn him over somehow, that it wouldn't be long.

I dug a deep hole in the sand beside him. I would lever him up and topple him in. I drove the spar into the sand underneath his shell. I drove it in again and again, until it was as deep as I could get it. I hauled back on it and felt him shift. I threw all my weight on it and at last he tumbled over into the hole, and the right way up, too. But when I scrambled over to him, his head lay limp in the sand, his eyes closed to the world. There wasn't a flicker of life about him. He was dead. I was quite sure of it now. It's silly, I know - I had only known him for a few minutes - but I felt I had lost a friend.

I made a pillow of soft sea lettuce for his head and knelt beside him. I cried till there were no more tears to cry. And then I saw the gulls were back. They knew too. I screamed at them, but they just glared at me and moved in closer.

'No!' I cried. 'No!'

I would never let them have him, never. I piled a mountain of seaweed on top of him and my driftwood on top of that. The next tide would take him away. I left him and went home.

I went back to Rushy Bay this evening, at high tide, just before nightfall, to see if my turtle was gone. He was still there. The high tide had not been high enough. The gulls were gone though, all of them. I really don't know what made me want to see his face once more. I pulled the wood and seaweed away until I could see the top of his head. As I looked it moved and lifted. He was blinking up at me. He was alive again! I could have kissed him, really I could. But I didn't quite dare.

He's still there now, all covered up against the gulls, I hope. In the morning...

I had to stop writing because Father just came in. He hardly ever comes in my room, so I knew at once something was wrong.

'You all right?' he said, standing in the doorway. 'What've you been up to?'

'Nothing', I said. 'Why?'

'Old man Jenkins. He said he saw you down on Rushy Bay.'

'I was just collecting the wood,' I told him, as calmly as I could, 'like you said I should.' I find lying so difficult. I'm just not good at it.

'He thought you were crying, crying your eyes out, he says.'

'I was not,' I said, but I dared not look at him. I pretended to go on writing in my diary.

'You are telling me the truth, Laura?' He knew I wasn't, he knew it.

'Course,' I said. I just wished he would go.

'What do you find to write in that diary of yours?' he asked.

'Things,' I said. 'Just things.'

And he went out and shut the door behind him. He knows something, but he doesn't know what. I'm going to have to be very careful. If Father finds out about the turtle, I'm in trouble. He's only got to go down to Rushy Bay and look. That turtle would just be food to him, and to anyone else who finds him. We're all hungry, everyone is getting hungrier every day. I should tell him. I know I should. But I can't do it. I just can't let them eat him.

In the morning, early, I'll have to get him back into the sea. I don't know how I'm going to do it, but somehow I will. I must. Now it's not only the gulls I have to save him from.

Michael Morpurgo

WORD BANK

bombarded attacked by throwing a lot of things
hauled pulled or dragged with difficulty
sea lettuce a kind of seaweed

spar a strong pole, used to make part of a ship
wizened shrivelled-looking

Language questions

1 This story is written as a diary. Write down a phrase from the text that shows:
a) it uses first-person narrative style (1)
b) it is written in the past tense.

2 Find an example of:
a) a compound sentence, suggesting an informal style. (3)
b) a contraction to create a more informal style
   e.g. we + are (formal) = we're (informal)

3 In a story, writers often use discourse markers to move the story forward – for example, 'later', 'next', 'then', 'after...' See if you can find examples of how the diary is organized. Are there any obvious discourse markers? (3)

4 Pick out some examples of unfamiliar words in the text (words you don't know or have not met before). These will be useful for a comparison task later.

5 Look up the words from the extract on the next page in a dictionary, to find out whether they are originally Old English or from Latin.
This will be at the end of the definition and abbreviated, for example:

habitation ME f. OF f. L *habitatio*

The last entry here is L for Latin: the word is initially from Latin.

but

house OE *hus* f. Gmc

counts as Old English.

- ▶ leatherback
- ▶ collect
- ▶ plenty
- ▶ worshipping
- ▶ wrinkled

You may need to divide some of the words into parts and look up the parts separately (e.g. 'leather' and 'back' for 'leatherback'). You could work with a partner to do this.

Using the information you have collected, say how much the text is written in formal or informal language. Use a number on this scale to show your decision:

very informal ____1 ____2 ____3 ____4 ____5 **very formal**

Does the style of the text feel like a real diary? Write two or three paragraphs saying whether it does or does not, commenting on text-, sentence-, and word-level features (see Language focus) to support your ideas.

Comprehension

1 Where did Laura find the turtle?

2 What did she think it was before she recognized it was a turtle?

3 Does she think the turtle is male or female?

4 Look more closely at the first paragraph. Does Laura show any emotion about finding the turtle, or is she just matter-of-fact? How can you tell?

5 Laura uses a simile to describe the turtle's appearance: 'like a two hundred year old man...' What does this show about her feelings for the creature?

6 By the middle of the extract Laura is writing about 'my turtle'. Why do you think she feels so attached to him?

7 What clues are there in the text that Laura is fascinated by the turtle?

8 The text takes place at three different times:
- when Laura finds the turtle
- later, when she returns to see how he is
- later still, when she is at home writing her diary.

How does the writer show us that time has passed?

9 Why do you think Laura won't say much to her father about her diary?

(3)

10 The final paragraph hints at trouble ahead. What do you think will happen next?

Extended response

What impression do we gain of Laura from this extract?

What do we learn about:
- her family
- where she lives
- her attitude to the turtle?

Write a detailed paragraph explaining what she is like. Aim to include some examples from the text to illustrate your points.

(5)

Speaking and listening

Pairs

When we speak to different people, we change the way we use language. For example, the way you speak to a teacher will be different from talking to your best friend. You may use different words, use a more formal structure, and perhaps change your accent.

Changing our language in different situations is known as register. In some situations we might use a formal register. In others we will use an informal register.

Take the extract about Laura discovering the turtle and practise re-telling it using different registers. Work in pairs on this activity. One of you plays the speaker. The other plays the listener, giving feedback on the way the speaker uses language. Then change roles for the next situation.

The table below gives you further guidance.

You are	Your audience is	The situation is	Your register is
1 Laura	Your class at school	You have been asked to give a class talk, so you tell them about finding the turtle.	Formal – a monologue (one person speaking) rather than a conversation; speaking to a large group; structured rather than spontaneous
2 Laura	Your best friend	You have just met your friend on your way home. You tell her/him about the turtle you have just found.	Informal, breathless, spontaneous, unstructured
3 Laura	A police officer	You fear that someone may try to hurt the turtle if you leave it on its own. You are asking the police officer for help.	Formal, courteous, hurried, urgent, worried

Now, again in pairs, discuss which of these contexts would be:

▶ most formal   ▶ most polite
▶ most informal   ▶ most structured.

Think of some specific words you might use in one context which you would be unlikely to use in another.

TEXT B

Born in 1660, shortly before the great plague and fire of London, Daniel Defoe was a journalist and novelist. He is often referred to as the first novelist in the English language, and he also established one of the earliest newspapers, in 1703. With over 500 publications to his name, Defoe must be one of the writers with the highest output of different texts.

Although it is sometimes described as the first novel in English, Defoe's novel *Robinson Crusoe* was in fact based on a true-life story. Alexander Selkirk was a sailor who went to sea in 1704, was put ashore on a Pacific island, and survived until he was rescued in 1709. Daniel Defoe expands the story. Robinson Crusoe is shipwrecked and manages to survive on his island for 28 years. In this extract he is exploring a different part of the island from where he has set up home, and is studying its wildlife...

Robinson Crusoe

AS SOON AS I CAME TO THE SEA SHORE, I was surprized to see that I had taken up my lot on the worst side of the island; for here indeed the shore was covered with innumerable turtles, whereas on the other side I had found but three in a year and half. Here was also an infinite number of fowls of many kinds, some which I had seen and some which I had not seen before, and many of them very good meat; but such as I knew not the names of, except those called penguins.

I could have shot as many as I pleased, but was very sparing of my powder and shot: and therefore had more mind to kill a she goat, if I could, which I could better feed on; and though there were many goats here more than on my side the island, yet it was with much more difficulty that I could come near them, the country being flat and even, and they saw me much sooner than when I was on the hill.

I confess this side of the country was much pleasanter than mine, but yet I had not the least inclination to remove; for as I was fixed in my habitation, it became natural to me, and I seemed all the while I was here to be as it were upon a journey, and from home. However, I travelled along the shore of the sea towards the east, I suppose about twelve miles; and then setting up a great pole upon the shore for a mark, I concluded I would go home again; and that the next journey I took should be on the other side of the island, east from my dwelling, and so round till I came to my post again; of which in its place.

I took another way to come back than that I went, thinking I could easily keep all the island so much in my view that I could not miss finding my first dwelling by viewing the country; but I found my self mistaken; for being come about two or three miles, I found my self descended into a very large valley; but so surrounded with hills, and those hills covered with wood, that I could not see which was my way by any direction but that of the sun, nor even then, unless I knew very well the position of the sun at that time of the day.

It happened to my farther misfortune, that the weather proved hazey for three or four days while I was in this valley; and not being able to see the sun, I wandered about very uncomfortably, and at last was obliged to find out the sea side, look for my post, and come back the same way I went; and then by easy journies I turned homeward, the weather being exceeding hot, and my gun, ammunition, hatchet, and other things very heavy.

In this journey my dog surprized a young kid, and seized upon it, and I running in to take hold of it, caught it, and saved it alive from the dog. I had a great mind to bring it home if I could; for I had often been musing whether it might not be possible to get a kid or two, and so raise a breed of tame goats, which might supply me when my powder and shot should be all spent.

I made a collar to this little creature, and with a string which I made of some rope–yarn, which I always carry'd about me, I led him along, tho' with some difficulty, till I came to my bower, and there I enclosed him and left him; for I was very impatient to be at home, from whence I had been absent above a month.

Daniel Defoe

WORD BANK

above a month more than a month
bower building surrounded by trees
dwelling a house or home
enclosed shut in
exceeding very
fowls birds

habitation a place to live, a house
hazey misty
infinite very large
innumerable too many to count
musing wondering
obliged to forced to
of which in its place more about this when I come to it

powder and shot gunpowder and bullets, ammunition
remove move house
seized upon pounced on
sparing of careful not to use too much of
whereas while

Comparison

1
a) What surprises Robinson Crusoe about this side of the island?
b) Why does he decide not to kill any of the birds?
c) What does he do with the goat he finds?

2
What does Robinson assume about the island at the beginning of paragraph 4?
How is he proved wrong?

3
How does Robinson hope to find his way in the hills? What stops him?

4
How does he find his way home in the end?

5
The text was written more than 250 years before *The Wreck of the Zanzibar*. What clues can you find to show that it is an old text? Look for five examples of words we probably wouldn't use much nowadays.

6
The Wreck of the Zanzibar uses a mix of sentence types, including complex and compound. Choose one paragraph of *Robinson Crusoe* and write down what type the sentences are – simple, compound or complex.

7
Use a dictionary to look up the words listed on the next page, and find out whether they are Old English or from Latin. (You have already done this for words from *The Wreck of the Zanzibar*: see pages 101-102 for a reminder of how to do this.)

▶ innumerable   ▶ inclination

▶ infinite   ▶ habitation

▶ fowls

You could work with a partner to do this.

 Overall, is this story more or less formal than *The Wreck of the Zanzibar*? Where would you place it on the informal/formal scale used on page 102? Explain why.

(Hint) Your answer to Language question 4 could be useful here.

 In *The Wreck of the Zanzibar*, Laura is concerned and worried about the well-being of the turtle. She is determined to look after him. What impression do you get of Robinson Crusoe's character and his attitude to nature? Use a table like this to compare what the two characters are like:

Laura	Robinson
What she is like:	What he is like:
Her attitude to nature:	His attitude to nature:

Writing assignments

1 Write a five-day diary describing your experiences in one of these situations.

Option A: You have crashed in an icy polar region. You are able to survive because you find an old abandoned iron hut with a small stove – a place where explorers have obviously made camp. There are blankets, and a little dried food, plus some basic equipment. How will you survive for five days before being rescued?

Use this sequence of events to help structure your story:

▶ waking up from the crash

- finding shelter
- a blizzard sets in
- mysteriously, overnight, some food is stolen – by an animal or human?
- what happens next?

Option B: You have been shipwrecked on a desert island on which you encounter some strange creatures but no human beings.

Use this structure:

- waking up after the shipwreck – first impressions of the island
- finding shelter and eating your first meal
- evening comes – and you sense the presence of some strange creatures
- what happens next?

Write your adventures using a diary format (look back at page 97 for a reminder of diary form). The first day's entry should describe the crash or shipwreck. The fifth day should describe your rescue.

2 Look again at the style of *Robinson Crusoe*, written all those years ago. How would you retell the story in a modern diary like Laura's? How would the vocabulary, sentences and structure be different? (Look back at the Language focus on pages 95-97 for hints on different kinds of sentence and think about how you might make the diary less formal.)

Have a go at rewriting it as a modern diary. Then write a paragraph describing the kinds of language changes you have made. Be as specific as you can about these, giving examples of words and phrases you cut, replaced or updated.

3 Fiction
Powers of description

Aims

In this unit you will:
- explore the way writers use language to create powerful settings
- compare the effects of verbs, adjectives and adverbs in creating description
- look at description in scientific writing
- use description in a spoken task
- write your own piece of descriptive writing.

Language focus

Writers use a number of techniques to help us imagine the people and places they are describing.

Adjectives and adverbs
Sometimes these refer to the **different senses** (sight, sound, touch/feeling, taste, smell):

> The walls were green, covered with furry moss in which tiny humming insects nested. The air was sweet with musty decay.

This often involves using **adjectives**:

green: sight   sweet: taste
furry: touch/feeling   musty: smell
humming: sound

Sometimes, writers use adverbs to show what is happening:

> Water dripped slowly down the walls.

Active and stative verbs
Instead of adjectives and adverbs, authors can use active verbs to bring their descriptions to life:

> Brick walls turn mossgreen. Pepper vines snake up electric poles

These are dynamic verbs: they describe something that is happening.

The writer might have used stative verbs:

> The walls are mossgreen. There are pepper vines on the electric poles.

Stative verbs describe processes where there is no obvious action. Other examples are:

seem   appear   think   hope   wait

TEXT A

Read the opening of this novel by Arundhati Roy and explore the way she makes her descriptions of people and places visual and powerful.

Arundhati Roy trained as an architect, and then worked as a production designer on several films. She lives in New Delhi. *The God of Small Things* is her first novel.

The God of Small Things

MAY IN AYEMENEM IS A HOT, BROODING MONTH. The days are long and humid. The river shrinks and black crows gorge on bright mangoes in still, dustgreen trees. Red bananas ripen. Jackfruits burst. Dissolute bluebottles hum vacuously in the fruity air. Then they stun themselves against clear windowpanes and die, fatly baffled in the sun.

The nights are clear but suffused with sloth and sullen expectation.

But by early June the south-west monsoon breaks and there are three months of wind and water with short spells of sharp, glittering sunshine that thrilled children snatch to play with. The countryside turns an immodest green. Boundaries blur as tapioca fences take root and bloom. Brick walls turn mossgreen. Pepper vines snake up electric poles. Wild creepers burst through laterite banks and spill across the flooded roads. Boats ply in the bazaars. And small fish appear in the puddles that fill the PWD potholes on the highways.

It was raining when Rahel came back to Ayemenem. Slanting silver ropes slammed into loose earth, ploughing it up like gun-fire. The old house on the hill wore its steep, gabled roof pulled over its ears like a low hat. The walls, streaked with moss, had grown soft, and bulged a little with dampness that seeped up from the ground. The wild, overgrown garden was full of the whisper and scurry of small lives. In the undergrowth a rat snake rubbed itself against a glistening stone. Hopeful yellow bullfrogs cruised the scummy pond for mates. A drenched mongoose flashed across the leaf-strewn driveway.

The house itself looked empty. The doors and windows were locked. The front verandah bare. Unfurnished. But the skyblue Plymouth with chrome tailfins was still parked outside, and inside, Baby Kochamma was still alive.

She was Rahel's baby grand aunt, her grandfather's younger sister. Her name was really Navomi, Navomi Ipe, but everybody called her Baby. She became Baby Kochamma when she was old enough to be an aunt. Rahel hadn't come to see her, though. Neither niece nor baby grand aunt laboured under any illusion on that account. Rahel had come to see her brother, Estha. They were two-egg twins. 'Dizygotic' doctors called them. Born from separate but simultaneously fertilized eggs. Estha – Esthappen – was the older by eighteen minutes.

They never did look much like each other, Estha and Rahel, and even when they were thin-armed children, flat-chested, worm-ridden and Elvis Presley-puffed, there was none of the usual 'Who is who?' and 'Which is which?' from oversmiling relatives or the Syrian Orthodox Bishops who frequently visited the Ayemenem house for donations.

The confusion lay in a deeper, more secret place.

In those early amorphous years when memory had only just begun, when life was full of Beginnings and no Ends, and Everything was For Ever, Esthappen and Rahel thought of themselves together as Me, and separately, individually, as We or Us. As though they were a rare breed of Siamese twins, physically separate, but with joint identities.

Now, these years later, Rahel has a memory of waking up one night giggling at Estha's funny dream.

Arundhati Roy

WORD BANK

dissolute greedy, thrill-seeking
gabled roof a sloping roof whose
 ends make a triangle
gorge on eat greedily
laboured under any illusions
 had any silly ideas

laterite a kind of clay
mongoose a small cat-like animal
 that kills snakes
ply move regularly among
PWD Public Works Department
scurry hurried movement

seeped up oozed up
sloth laziness
suffused with mixed with
sullen sulky
vacuously aimlessly, stupidly

Language questions

 1 Arundhati Roy uses various techniques to bring her story to life.
Look at the first paragraph. Find the following:
a) two adjectives associated with the sense of sight
b) two adjectives associated with feeling
c) two adverbs
d) two active verbs
e) one stative verb.

 2 Some people like description in texts. It helps them to visualize or
imagine a scene. Other people get impatient – they want the story
to keep moving.
a) Look at paragraph 4, 'It was raining...' to '... driveway'.
 Experiment with what happens if you take out some of the
 descriptive writing from the paragraph. How does it feel if you
 delete the adjectives, so that 'slanting silver ropes slammed into
 loose earth' becomes 'ropes slammed into the earth'?

Have a go at rewriting the paragraph, cutting back as much of
the descriptive language as you can. You may need to add
determiners like 'a' and 'the' to make your version read properly.
b) Compare your rewritten version with a friend's. Write a
 paragraph about how the story feels different in its new version.

 3 Now explore the writer's use of the senses in greater detail. Which
senses does she refer to and which does she leave out?
Put phrases from the text into a table like the one on the next page,
to show which senses are referred to (a few have been done to start
you off):

Sight	Sound	Smell	Taste	Feeling
black	bluebottles hum			humid

Be ready to report your findings back to the rest of the class and see if their survey of the text revealed the same answers.

 4 The writer uses some vocabulary which surprises or even confuses us. For example, she modifies nouns using unexpected adjectives (example 1) and modifies adjectives with surprising adverbs (example 2). Look at the examples below. For each one, try to say what picture it creates in your mind.

Image	Picture in your mind
1 fruity air	
2 fatly baffled	
3 Elvis Presley-puffed	
4 immodest green	
5 oversmiling relatives	

 5 The writer's descriptions are often powerful because they use simile and metaphor to compare one thing with another. These devices help writers to create a picture of what they are describing.

Look at these similes. For each one, try to describe the impression given by the simile or metaphor. Give as much detail as possible about the picture the comparison creates in your mind.

a) The metaphor 'slanting silver ropes of rain' creates this picture of the rain: _____

b) The simile 'ploughing up the earth like gunfire' creates this impression of the earth: _____

c) The simile 'house wore its roof pulled down over its ears like an old hat' creates this impression of the roof: _____

 6 The writer uses some very short sentences in the first paragraph (e.g. 'Jackfruits burst'). What effect do these have?

Comprehension

1 Look more closely at the first paragraph. Write down three clues that the novel is not set in Britain.

2 How does the landscape change in early June?

3 What is the skyblue Plymouth?

4 Read paragraph 3 again. What happens when the rain comes? How does the writer make this feel lively and active?

Hint Look at the verbs, especially in the second half of the paragraph.

5 Look at paragraphs 4 and 5, which describe the house and its garden.

How do you think Rahel sees the house? Pick two adjectives from the list and write a paragraph to explain why you have chosen them. Give reasons from the text.

- sad
- neglected
- decaying
- welcoming
- lively
- forbidding

6 The writer says that the twins were like

> a rare breed of Siamese twins, physically separate, but with joint identities

Say in your own words what you think she means.

7 Does the text suggest what might happen next in the story? Why is it hard to predict the next stage?

Extended response

How does the writer use language to create a vivid picture of the setting?

You might mention her use of:
- sensuous words (covering the different senses)
- combinations of unusual words
- variety of kinds of sentence.

TEXT B

Description can also be a vital part of non-fiction texts. Here is an extract from some seventeenth-century science writing. This was a period when a fascination with science led to some remarkable discoveries, the period when:

▶ the first pendulum clock was invented
▶ the human nervous system was discovered
▶ the moon's orbit was measured for the first time.

Here Robert Hooke, an astronomer and naturalist, describes what he sees when he looks through the microscope he invented at the hunting spider.

The hunting spider

The hunting spider is a small grey spider, prettily bespecked with black spots all over its body, which the microscope discovers to be a kind of feathers, like those on butterflies' wings or the body of the white moth. Its gait is very nimble, by fits, sometimes running and sometimes leaping, like a grasshopper almost, then standing still and setting itself on its hinder legs. It will very nimbly turn its body and look round itself every way. It has six very conspicuous eyes, two looking directly forwards, placed just before; two other, on either side of those, looking forwards and sideways; and two other about the middle of the top of its back or head, which look backwards and sidewards. These seemed to be the biggest. The surface of them all was very black, spherical, purely polished, reflecting a very clear and distinct image of all the ambient objects, such as a window, a man's hand, a white paper, or the like.

Robert Hooke

Comparison

 1   Here is a quick sketch of the hunting spider. Copy it out. Using the information in Text B, write captions about the main features which are labelled. Write down what the writer tells us about the parts of the spider pointed at by the arrows.

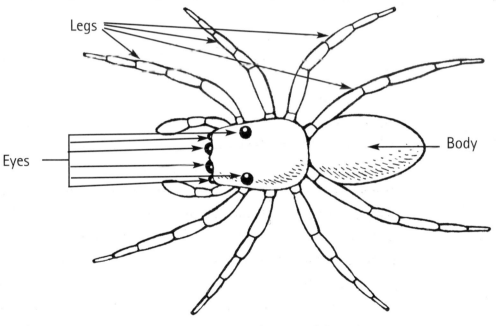

Legs

Eyes

Body

 2   Look more closely at the way the writer describes the spider. Find two examples each of:
- ▶ adjectives
- ▶ adverbs.

3   Does the writer use words which are connected to the senses? Which senses are referred to? Fill in the chart with words and phrases from the text, as you did with Text A.

Sight	Smell	Texture	Taste	Sound

Now look at the verbs in the text. Here they are listed in the order they are used.

a) Look back at the text to see how they are used in context. Then, for each one, decide whether it is dynamic or stative (see Language focus, page 110):

Verb	Dynamic or stative?
Is	
Discovers	
Running	
Leaping	
Standing still	
Setting itself	
Will turn	
Look round	
Has	
Looking	
Placed	
Seemed to be	
Was	
Reflecting	

b) Are the verbs mostly dynamic, mostly stative, or evenly mixed?

Look again at the two texts. Which one gives you the clearest picture of what is being described? Explain why, using words and sentences from the text to support your answer.

Speaking and listening

Class/group

Now see what your own descriptive powers are like. This activity works best with a set of objects which you will be asked to describe in detail. For example:

▶ stones of similar size
▶ exercise books of the same colour
▶ a set of old textbooks
▶ pieces of chalk.

You can do this as a class or small group activity. Each person is given one item – a piece of chalk, a stone, etc. You have two minutes to get to know its shape, texture and appearance in detail – just by looking at it. Make notes as you do this.

Then your item is placed with four or five others. In turn, using your notes, you describe what your object is like. Just like Robert

Hooke's detailed scientific description, you should try to give a very detailed factual account. Others in your group see if they can identify your object based on your description.

Then give each other feedback on how well you described the object.

Some hints:

▶ Start with more general features first. These help people to narrow down which object it might be – for example, mention size and colour before talking about specific marks or blemishes it might have.
▶ Use your notes as a guide but try not to just read them out. Make eye-contact with your audience and avoid looking at the object you are describing.

Writing assignments

1 One pleasure of Arundhati Roy's writing is its lively, creative style. It is as if she sees the world afresh for the first time, rather like the writing of Dylan Thomas, Salman Rushdie and Charles Dickens.

Use a setting you know well – perhaps the room you are sitting in now. Use it as the opening for a novel, but describe it using unexpected, vivid language. You might:

▶ focus on different senses (you can use adjectives for this – look back at the Language focus on p110 for some examples to remind you how)
▶ place unexpected words side by side (but remember the point is to give a clear picture, not just to surprise; look at your answers to Language question 4, to remind yourself how Arundhati Roy does this)
▶ use short and long sentences to create variety.

Aim to make the scene come alive, introducing a character into the scene after three paragraphs – someone perhaps sitting where you are or suddenly looking into the room.

2 Imagine you are writing for someone who has just arrived on planet Earth from a distant world. You have been asked to write a guide to everyday life.

Choose one process that we usually take for granted – for example, cleaning our teeth, making coffee, making a telephone call.

Describe the process in detail, telling your audience about the tools involved (toothbrush, toothpaste, taps, etc.), and how the process works.

Hints

▷ Think about the structure of your writing. It might be useful to organize it into subheadings:

> Aim:
> Equipment:
> Process:

▷ Think about the best tone to use. It might be worth experimenting with the second person mode: *First you need a toothbrush.*
Or perhaps it's better to make it as impersonal as possible:
A toothbrush is a plastic stick with white bristles arranged at one end...

▷ Focus on descriptive writing so that your account is detailed and very specific. Look again at Text B to see how Robert Hooke does this.

▷ Avoid using imperative verbs ('Pour water in the kettle... switch the kettle on') because these will make it sound too much like a list of instructions. You are aiming to explain rather than to instruct.

1 Poetry
Ballads old and new

Aims

In this unit you will:
- learn about the ballad's history and poetic form
- study an old ballad and a modern one
- investigate how words in the English language have changed over time
- hold a debate about a character in a ballad
- write your own ballad.

Language focus

A ballad is a simple song or poem which tells a story – a type of narrative poem. Ballads usually tell of the lives of popular folk heroes, both real and mythical, and often at great length – some of the Robin Hood ballads have more than ninety verses! Ballads usually focus on the more sensational aspects of life – supernatural happenings, violence, scandal, forbidden love or the exploits of infamous criminals – rather like the tabloid newspapers of today.

Ballads have been composed for many centuries – some probably date from the twelfth and thirteenth centuries. They were part of ordinary people's culture. At a time when the vast majority of people in Britain could not read or write, they passed down stories from generation to generation by word of mouth. Ballads were stories or songs composed to be spoken or sung aloud, rather than written down.

Ballads often changed over time. New verses might be added or old ones removed, as each new person who told or sang the ballad would adapt it a little, or remember it slightly differently.

Ballad form

The traditional folk ballad form varies but usually includes these features:

- regular stanzas of four lines each
- line 2 rhyming with line 4
- a strong, regular rhythm
- simple language – words of one or two syllables
- repetition or a refrain
- simple direct speech
- a minimum of description
- impersonal third-person narrative viewpoint (e.g. 'He went/They went' not 'I went')

These features make ballads easier to remember and learn by heart.

Rhythm and rhyme

Techniques of rhyme and rhythm can also be used to help make poetry easier to remember, so they are often used in ballads. Here are some of the terms that you will be using in this unit.

Full rhyme Rhyming words whose end sounds match exactly, e.g.

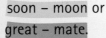

soon – moon or
great – mate.

End rhyme When the last words of lines of poetry are the rhyming words.

Stanza A separate, distinct group of lines in a poem.

Repetition The repeating of a line, phrase or word within a poem.

Refrain A line repeated at intervals throughout the ballad.

Rhyme scheme Many poems have rhyming lines. The pattern in which rhyming lines occur in a poem is called its **rhyme scheme**. If you are describing a poem's rhyme scheme, you usually use letters of the alphabet to show which lines rhyme with which others. Each different rhyme is given a different letter:

> I wander'd lonely as a cloud (a)
> That floats on high o'er vales and hills (b)
> When all at once I saw a crowd (a)
> A host of golden daffodils (b)
> Beside the lake, beneath the trees (c)
> Fluttering and dancing in the breeze. (c)

In this stanza from William Wordsworth's famous poem *The Daffodils*, the rhyme scheme is ababcc – line 1 rhymes with line 3; line 2 rhymes with line 4 and lines 5 and 6 rhyme. Lines 5 and 6 form a **rhyming couplet** (a pair of rhyming lines together).

Rhythm A difference between poetry and prose is that poems often have a more regular or obvious rhythm. The term 'rhythm' is used to refer to the pattern of beats created by the words in a poem and the way they are organized. Some words or syllables are emphasized more than others. For example, in the three-syllable word 'se̲cretary', we emphasize (or stress) the first syllable more than the others. If you read out loud the first two lines of *The Daffodils*, you can hear that we stress certain syllables naturally:

> I wander'd lonely as a cloud
> That floats on high o'er vales and hills.

Language change

The English language is a living language which has changed and developed over time and continues to do so. Language change is a vast topic and we can only just begin to look at it here.

There are four main kinds of language change:
- changes in the grammar
- changes in the words used
- changes in the meaning of words
- changes in how we pronounce words.

Changes in the words used are the most noticeable form of language change in English. Some words (sometimes called **archaic** words or **archaisms**) have died out altogether, while new words are always being added to the language. Even when words remain, it is common for them to change their <u>meaning</u> over time, e.g. the word 'nice' has changed meaning almost too many times to count. It has in turn meant 'silly', 'fussy', 'precise', and now 'pleasant'.

TEXT A

The early Scottish ballad *Sir Patrick Spens* was first published in written form in 1765 in *Reliques of Ancient English Poetry*, a collection of ancient ballads, sonnets and historical songs. It includes lots of old words, which may be unfamiliar to you. Not all of these are in the Word bank, as Language questions 1 and 2 will help you work through them.

Its original creator is unknown.

Sir Patrick Spens

The king sits in Dunfermline town
Drinking the blude-red wine;
'O where will I get a skeely skipper
To sail this new ship o' mine?'

O up and spake an eldern knight,
Sat at the king's right knee:
'Sir Patrick Spens is the best sailor
That ever sail'd the sea.'

Our king has written a broad letter,
And seal'd it with his hand,
And sent it to Sir Partrick Spens,
Was walking on the strand.

'To Noroway, to Noroway,
To Noroway o'er the foam;
The king's daughter o' Noroway,
'Tis thou must bring her home.'

The first word that Sir Patrick read
So loud, loud laugh'd he;
The next word that Sir Patrick read
The tear blinded his e'e.

'O who is this has done this deed
And told the king o' me,
To send us out, at this time o' year,
To sail upon the sea?

'Be it wind, be it wet, be it hail, be it sleet,
Our ship must sail the foam;
The king's daughter o' Noroway,
'Tis we must fetch her home.'

They hoisted their sails on Monenday morn
With all the speed they may;
They have landed in Noroway
Upon a Wednesday.

Sir Patrick Spens and his men are insulted by the Norwegians who suggest the Scots have outstayed their welcome. They sail for home immediately without waiting for good weather.

'Make ready, make ready, my merry men all!
Our good ship sails the morn.' –
'Now ever alack, my master dear,
I fear a deadly storm.

'I saw the new moon late yest'r-e'en
With the old moon in her arm;
And if we go to sea, master,
I fear we'll come to harm.'

They had not sail'd a league, a league,
A league but barely three,
When the lift grew dark, and the wind blew
   loud,
And gurly grew the sea.

The anchors brake, and the topmast lap,
It was such a deadly storm;
And the waves came o'er the broken ship
Till all her sides were torn.

'O where will I get a good sailor
To take my helm in hand,
While I go up to the tall topmast
To see if I can spy land?' –

'O here am I, a sailor good,
To take the helm in hand,
While you go up to the tall topmast,
But I fear you'll ne'er spy land.'

He had not gone a step, a step,
A step but barely one,
When a bolt flew out of our goodly ship,
And the salt sea it came in.

'Go fetch a web o' the silken cloth,
Another o' the twine,
And wap them into our ship's side,
And let not the sea come in.'

They fetch'd a web o' the silken cloth,
Another o' the twine,
And they wapp'd them round that good ship's
   side,
But still the sea came in.

O loth, loth were our good Scots lords
To wet their cork-heel'd shoon;
But long ere all the play was play'd
They wet their hats aboon.

And many was the feather bed
That flatter'd on the foam;
And many was the good lord's son
That never more came home.

O long, long may the ladies sit,
With their fans into their hand,
Before they see Sir Patrick Spens
Come sailing to the strand!

And long, long may the maidens sit
With their gold combs in their hair,
A-waiting for their own dear loves!
For them they'll see no more.

Half-o'er, half-o'er to Aberdour,
'Tis fifty fathoms deep;
And there lies good Sir Patricks Spens,
With the Scots lords at his feet!

Anonymous

WORD BANK

Aberdour old name for the Scottish city of Aberdeen

Dunfermline Scottish city where many ancient Scottish kings are buried

ere before

fathom a measure for depth of water, equal to six feet

flatter'd fluttered

half o'er halfway across the sea

helm steering apparatus of a boat or ship

lap flew apart, broke

league a measure of distance, about 3 miles

lift sky

new moon... with the old moon in her arms a crescent moon behind which you can see the whole moon; sailors thought this was a sign of a bad storm

Noroway Norway

spy see

strand a beach

twine string

Language questions

1   *Sir Patrick Spens* contains many examples of words which are no longer in use in modern English. These words are either old dialect words or archaic words. Look at the following list of words from the poem:

blude-red	e'e	o'er	gurly
skeely	Monenday	loth	wap
spake	Alack	shoon	
eldern	yest'r-e'en	aboon	

From the list, find the following:

a) The archaic plural of the word 'shoe'.

b) A different spelling of a word still in use.

c) The archaic past tense form of the verb 'speak'.

d) An abbreviated word.

2   For the other words in the list given in question 1, try to give their meaning or spelling in modern English. (You might like to discuss this with a partner.)

3   Earlier in this unit you read about the history and poetic features of ballads.

a) How many lines are there in each stanza of this ballad?

b) The chart lists some features of traditional ballads. Copy it out and give an example of each feature from *Sir Patrick Spens*.

Feature of ballad	Examples from text
Repetition	
End rhyme	
Use of direct speech	

4   Look again at the first three stanzas of the poem. Using the lettering method explained on page 122, how would you describe the rhyme scheme of the poem?

5   a) Read the first four stanzas of the poem again. Count the

number of syllables in each line. Do they all have the same
number of syllables?
Now compare the stanzas with each other. Does the number of
syllables in different lines fall into a pattern across the stanzas?

b) Ballads usually have a strong, regular rhythm (see Language
focus, page 122). Read the same four stanzas again, this time
trying to get a feel for the rhythm.
Count the number of stresses in the lines. Is there a pattern to
the stresses?
Hint Watch out for the third line – the pattern here may vary
between stanzas.

c) Copy out the stanza below. Try to decide where you would mark
the stressed syllables. The first line has been done to help you.
Hint You may need to think quite carefully about lines whose
number of syllables can change from stanza to stanza.

O who is this has done this deed

And told the king o' me,

To send us out at this time o' year,

To sail upon the sea?

  What are the effects of the following examples of repetition from
the ballad?

a) 'They had not sail'd a league, a league,
A league but barely three' (stanza 11) and
'He had not gone a step, a step,
A step but barely one' (stanza 13)

b) 'O long, long may the ladies sit' (stanza 20) and
'And long, long may the maidens sit' (stanza 21)

Comprehension

1 At the top of the next page is a list of events from the story of *Sir
Patrick Spens*. They have been jumbled up. Read them carefully and

decide what is the right order. Then copy the points out in their correct order.

a) Sir Patrick Spens receives the letter as he is walking.

b) The women of the court wait in vain for the ship to return.

c) The king writes and seals the letter to Sir Patrick Spens.

d) The ship is caught in a storm in the North Sea and breaks up.

e) In Dunfermline, the king asks for a good captain to sail a ship and bring the Norwegian king's daughter home.

f) The ship sinks and all the men aboard are drowned.

g) Sir Patrick Spens gives instructions to prepare to leave Norway and return home.

h) The ship sails for Norway on a Monday morning.

2 What does the king want and why?

3 What image is created in stanza 1 by the king drinking 'blude-red wine'?

4 Look carefully at stanza 5.

a) Why do you think Sir Patrick Spens laughed loudly at the letter?

b) Why then has a tear 'blinded his e'e'?

Hint Look at the next two verses.

5 From stanzas 6 and 7, select the lines or phrases which show Sir Patrick's fears at having to do as the king asks.

6 Ballads often include omens, foretelling doom. Copy out the lines which relate a bad omen.

7 Pick out some words and phrases from stanzas 11 and 12 used to describe the weather and the sea conditions. What effects do these words have on the reader?

8 Look carefully again at stanzas 18 and 19. What do we learn about 'our good Scots lords' from these stanzas?

Hint Think especially about what you think 'their cork-heel'd shoon' and 'feather beds' show about their lifestyles.

Extended response

How is the poem 'Sir Patrick Spens' written to make its story exciting and make us want to read to the end?

Write an answer of 3-4 paragraphs, trying to include some specific words and phrases from the poem in your answer.

Use the points below to help you answer the question:
- How does Sir Patrick react when he reads the king's letter?
- How do we know he fears having to do as he is asked?
- How does the way the sea and the weather are described in the poem create a sense of danger?
- What do you feel when the crew member says he fears there will be a storm on the return journey?
- How does the repetition in the ballad help to increase the tension?

TEXT B

Elizabeth Bishop is an American poet who was born in Massachusetts in 1911. She travelled widely throughout her life, finally settling in Brazil. Her poetry reflects her interests in travel and different cultures. Her *Complete Poems*, published in 1983, appeared after her death in 1979.

The burglar in the ballad has a Portuguese name: Micuçú - pronounced Mick-u-<u>su</u>.

The Burglar of Babylon

On the fair green hills of Rio
There grows a fearful stain:
The poor who come to Rio
And can't go home again.

On the hills a million people,
A million sparrows, nest,
Like a confused migration
That's had to light and rest,

Building its nests, or houses,
Out of nothing at all, or air.
You'd think a breath would end them,
They perch so lightly there.

But they cling and spread like lichen,
And the people come and come.
There's one hill called the Chicken,
And one called Catacomb;

There's the hill of Kerosene,
And the hill of the Skeleton,
The hill of Astonishment,
And the hill of Babylon.

Micuçú was a burglar and killer,
An enemy of society.
He had escaped three times
From the worst penitentiary.

They don't know how many he murdered
(Though they say he never raped),
And he wounded two policemen
This last time he escaped.

They said, 'He'll go to his auntie,
Who raised him like a son.
She has a little drink shop
On the hill of Babylon.'

He did go straight to his auntie,
And he drank a final beer.
He told her, 'The soldiers are coming,
And I've got to disappear.

'Ninety years they gave me.
Who wants to live that long?
I'll settle for ninety hours,
On the hill of Babylon.

'Don't tell anyone you saw me.
I'll run as long as I can.
You were good to me, and I love you,
But I'm a doomed man.'

Going out, he met a *mulata*
Carrying water on her head.
'If you say you saw me, daughter,
You're just as good as dead.'

There are caves up there, and hideouts,
And an old fort, falling down.
They used to watch for Frenchmen
From the hill of Babylon.

Below him was the ocean.
It reached far up the sky,
Flat as a wall, and on it
Were freighters passing by,

Or climbing the wall, and climbing
Till each looked like a fly,
And then fell over and vanished;
And he knew he was going to die.

He could hear the goats *baa-baa*-ing,
He could hear the babies cry;
Fluttering kites strained upward;
And he knew he was going to die.

A buzzard flapped so near him
He could see its naked neck.
He waved his arms and shouted,
'Not yet, my son, not yet!'

An Army helicopter
Came nosing around and in.
He could see two men inside it,
But they never spotted him.

The soldiers were all over,
On all sides of the hill,
And right against the skyline
A row of them, small and still.

Children peeked out of windows,
And men in the drink shop swore,
And spat a little *cachaça*
At the light cracks in the floor.

But the soldiers were nervous, even
With tommy guns in hand,
And one of them, in a panic,
Shot the officer in command.

He hit him in three places;
The other shots went wild.
The soldier had hysterics
And sobbed like a little child.

The dying man said, 'Finish
The job we came here for.'
He committed his soul to God
And his sons to the Governor.

They ran and got a priest,
And he died in hope of Heaven
– A man from Pernambuco,
The youngest of eleven.

They wanted to stop the search,
But the Army said, 'No, go on,'
So the soldiers swarmed again
Up the hill of Babylon.

Rich people in apartments
Watched through binoculars
As long as the daylight lasted.
And all night, under the stars,

Micuçú hid in the grasses
Or sat in a little tree,
Listening for sounds, and staring
At the lighthouse out at sea.

And the lighthouse stared back at him,
Till finally it was dawn.
He was soaked with dew, and hungry,
On the hill of Babylon.

The yellow sun was ugly,
Like a raw egg on a plate –
Slick from the sea. He cursed it,
For he knew it sealed his fate.

He saw the long white beaches
And people going to swim,
With towels and beach umbrellas,
But the soldiers were after him.

Far, far below, the people
Were little colored spots,
And the heads of those in swimming
Were floating coconuts.

He heard the peanut vendor
Go *peep-peep* on his whistle,
And the man that sells umbrellas
Swinging his watchman's rattle.

Women with market baskets
Stood on the corners and talked,
Then went on their way to market,
Gazing up as they walked.

The rich with their binoculars
Were back again, and many
Were standing on the rooftops,
Among TV antennae.

It was early, eight or eight-thirty.
He saw a soldier climb,
Looking right at him. He fired,
And missed for the last time.

He could hear the soldier panting,
Though he never got very near.
Micuçú dashed for shelter.
But he got it, behind the ear.

He heard the babies crying
Far, far away in his head,
And the mongrels barking and barking.
Then Micuçú was dead.

He had a Taurus revolver,
And just the clothes he had on,
With two contos in the pockets,
On the hill of Babylon.

The police and the populace
Heaved a sigh of relief,
But behind the counter his auntie
Wiped her eyes in grief.

'We have always been respected.
My shop is honest and clean.
I loved him, but from a baby
Micuçú was always mean.

'We have always been respected.
His sister has a job.
Both of us gave him money.
Why did he have to rob?

'I raised him to be honest,
Even here, in Babylon slum.'
The customers had another,
Looking serious and glum.

But one of them said to another,
When he got outside the door,
'He wasn't much of a burglar,
He got caught six times – or more.'

This morning the little soldiers
Are on Babylon hill again;
Their gun barrels and helmets
Shine in a gentle rain.

Micuçú is buried already.
They're after another two,
But they say they aren't as dangerous
As the poor Micuçú.

On the fair green hills of Rio
There grows a fearful stain:
The poor who come to Rio
And can't go home again.

There's the hill of Kerosene,
And the hill of the Skeleton,
The hill of Astonishment,
And the hill of Babylon.

Elizabeth Bishop

WORD BANK

antennae aerials
Babylon a Biblical place, used to mean a place of sorrowful exile or decadence
cachaça a drink like rum
catacomb an underground tomb
committed gave to someone to care for

contos old coins
freighters cargo-carrying boats
kerosene paraffin oil
lichen a plant that usually grows on walls
migration a large number of people moving to live in another place

mulata a woman with coffee coloured skin
penitentiary a prison (U.S. word)
populace the common people
Rio Rio de Janeiro, a major city in Brazil
tommy gun a light machine-gun
vendor a person selling something

Comparison

1 Copy out the blank storyboard shown below. Then try to decide on eight pictures and eight captions which will illustrate the main stages of the narrative of *The Burglar of Babylon*. The captions can be short quotations from the poem or can be in your own words.

'On the hills a million people'.

Look carefully at stanzas 1–5 of *The Burglar of Babylon* which tell us a lot about the community Micuçú comes from and then answer the following questions:

a) What is the 'fearful stain' and what has caused it?

b) The poem compares the people who live on the hills to sparrows, and their makeshift homes to nests. What effect does this have?

The poem does not present Micuçú as either totally good or totally bad. Read through the poem carefully, completing the following lists of evidence about Micuçú.

Good	Bad
He 'never raped'	A burglar and a killer.
Tells his aunt, 'You were good to me and I love you'	'an enemy of society'

Using your evidence from question 3, what do you think the poet's view of Micuçú is? Is she sympathetic or unsympathetic to him, or a combination of both?

Although this ballad is mainly a narrative poem, it also seems to present a view of the society in which it is set.

a) What you think the poet feels about:

▶ the poor of Rio living on the hills?

▶ Micuçú's life?

▶ the officer who was accidentally killed?

▶ the rich people in their apartments watching the manhunt through their binoculars?

▶ Micuçú's aunt?

Find quotations in the poem to back up your opinion.

b) Read the following statements about the poem and decide which you most agree with and why:

▶ The poet wants us to feel that Micuçú is a cold-blooded murderer and a dangerous criminal who the police have to kill if necessary.

▶ The poet is sympathetic to the police and to the law-abiding citizens of Rio.

▶ The poet creates sympathy for the poor of Rio and shows us that Micuçú had little choice in life except to turn to crime.

Both *Sir Patrick Spens* and *The Burglar of Babylon* are examples of ballads which tell a story. However, they were created many centuries apart. What similarities can you find between the two poems? Make a list of as many as you can find. Here are a few examples to help you begin:

▶ Both poems tell a story.
▶ Both poems have a clear beginning, middle and ending.
▶ The endings of both poems involve death.
▶ Both poems have a main character: Sir Patrick Spens and Micuçú.

Hint In your answer, try to include points both about the stories told in the poems and about the ballad form.

The major difference between the two texts is the use of language in each. The language reflects the different historical times in which the ballads were composed. Find five words or phrases from Text B which show that the poem is modern and the story is set in the present.

Both ballads are narrative poems – they both tell a story. Which poem's story did you find the most enjoyable? Try to give three or four clear reasons to explain your choice.
You might like to think about:

▶ the settings for the poems
▶ the two main characters – Sir Patrick Spens and Micuçú
▶ the use of detail and language
▶ the events in the stories.

Speaking and listening

Class

As a class you are going to debate the question: 'Did Micuçú deserve to die?'
This is called the **motion** and is phrased in the following way:

> This House believes that Micuçú deserved to die.

Before the debate, the class will divide into two groups. One group will support the motion, finding arguments for why Micuçú deserved to die. The other group will find arguments against the motion. Spend some time in your groups, re-reading the poem to find evidence to support your group's viewpoint.

In the debate you will have the chance to give

your group's opinion and evidence, listen to the other group's ideas and challenge them if you want. Your teacher will act as the chairperson and will say who can speak. Remember, only one person should speak at a time.

Listen to others carefully. At the end, the chairperson will hold a vote to see how many people support the motion and agree that Micuçú deserved to die, and how many oppose it and do not believe he deserved to die. To vote, decide which side has really persuaded you; you don't have to stay with the side you were arguing for.

Writing assignments

1 Write your own modern ballad using the following guidelines to help you:

▷ Decide on a story. Traditional stories can make good topics – a myth, a religious story or a famous event from history. You may wish to choose a more contemporary story, either fictional or based on fact. Many ballads focus on the events surrounding one central character's life e.g. the Robin Hood ballads.

▷ Work out a plan for your ballad. Perhaps design a storyboard as you did for *The Burglar of Babylon*. Try to develop your story through 8-10 stanzas. For each stanza, write a few lines in rough describing where the story is set and what happens in it, e.g.

	Setting	What happens
Stanza 1	Playground	A tough gang from a rival school arrive

▷ Read again the two ballads in this unit. Work out 'the rules' of the ballad form. Copy out the paragraph below – you will need to fill in the gaps!

'In traditional ballads, the stanzas all have _____ lines. Lines _____ and _____ always rhyme. The number of syllables in each line is usually _____ throughout every stanza, creating a _____ sense of rhythm.' (The answers are at the bottom of the page.)

▶ Write the first draft of your ballad, trying to keep to the rules of the ballad form (for a reminder of other features of ballads, look back at p122). When you have finished your draft, read it aloud to a friend and ask them to suggest any changes or improvements you could make.

▶ When you are happy with any changes you have made to your ballad, write a final version and illustrate it.

2   Many ballads are based on true-life stories. For example, Charles Causley's poem, *The Ballad Of Charlotte Dymond*, is based on an actual nineteenth-century crime. Charlotte Dymond, a servant girl, was murdered by her sweetheart on 14 April, 1844 and her story is told in Causley's ballad.

Write an article for a tabloid newspaper based on the story of *Sir Patrick Spens* or *The Burglar of Babylon*. Remember the rules of newspaper reporting – you must answer the questions, who, where, what, why, how and when. Try to lay out your page like a newspaper's front page, with a bold headline, columns, and an illustration. (For a reminder of features of newspaper reports and how they are laid out, look back at the language focus in Non-fiction and media unit 1, on pages 6-7.)

Think of the ways you can use language to try to create a particular emotional response from your audience. For example, was Sir Patrick Spens a loyal, heroic subject, or a foolish man who should have refused the king when he realized he was putting the lives of his crew in danger? Was Micuçú a cold-hearted killer, or a local folk hero?

Poetry
Sound and shape

Aims

In this unit you will:

▶ study two poems by twentieth-century poets

▶ consider how the structure and layout of a poem contribute to its meaning

▶ focus on how sound patterns are used in poetry

▶ experiment with writing shape poems and changing the layouts of poems.

Language focus

There are many differences between poetry and prose. One of the most important is that poetry is much more concerned with the way words sound. Poetry often has strong rhythms, and uses rhyme and other sound patterns to create particular effects. The most common sound features are:

Alliteration

This is the term used to describe a series of words next to or near each other which all begin with the same sound. This creates particular sound effects, e.g. Wet, windy weather

Rhyme

Words rhyme when their end sounds match, e.g. eight – mate
Note: words that rhyme do not always have a similar spelling.

There are many different kinds of rhyme. Some of the most important are:

End rhyme When the last word of a line of poetry is the rhyming word.

Internal rhyme When a word in the middle of the line rhymes with the word at the end of the line.

Full rhyme When words rhyme completely, e.g. host – boast.

Half rhyme When words do not rhyme fully but their sounds are similar, e.g. town – stone.

TEXT A

. . . .

Edwin Morgan was born in Glasgow in 1920. He served in the Middle East with the Royal Army Medical Corps during World War Two and then returned to the University of Glasgow where he studied English Literature. He is a much-admired poet, translator and academic. Many of his poems are about the effects of new scientific or technological inventions and he is also well-known for using new and inventive forms for his poems. The following poem is a vivid description of a heron.

Heron

A gawky stilt-
ed fossicker a-
mong reeds, the
gun-grey-green
one, gauntly
watchful cold-
eye, stiff on
single column a
brooding hump
of wind-ruffled
feather-brain
feathering the
blue shall-
ows with one
scaly claw
poised drip-
ping –

wades
the pebbled lake,
prints the mudflat,
scorns the noi-
sy fancy oy-
stercatchers' talk,
stalks, tall, to
his flat ramshack-
le nest or shack
of slack sticks
with three dull
greeny eggs
by a bul-
rush grove –

till the snaky neck
coils back
and strikes, beak
darts and spears
quick fish,
fish, fish
silvery-rich
fisher-king dish –

and then in the lone-
ly white lazy
hazy afternoon
he rises slowly
in a big zig-
zag heavy over
sultry fens
and windmill vanes,
flapping silently
in the land of wings.

Edwin Morgan

WORD BANK

bulrush a water plant
fossicker a creature or person that searches or rummages
gauntly an adverb made from the adjective 'gaunt'; bonily ill - looking

gawky awkward, clumsy
oystercatcher a wading bird with an orange-coloured bill
poised composed, ready for action

ramshackle messy, rickety
sultry hot, humid
vane the arm of a windmill

Language questions

1 In the Language focus, you learnt about some of the ways poets create patterns of sound, and the terms used to describe these patterns. In *Heron*, the poet uses many kinds of sound patterns including these two features:
  ▶ alliteration
  ▶ repetition.
For each of them try to find at least two examples from the poem. An example is done for you.

Sound pattern	Example
Alliteration	1 'gun-grey-green' 2
Repetition	1 2

2 What different kinds of rhyme can you find in the poem? List as many examples as you can of each type.

(Hint) The poet splits a lot of words across lines. Look carefully at the ends of lines for rhymes.

3 Look at the last two stanzas of *Heron*. Try to read them out loud. Can you feel a change in pace between these two verses? Which one feels quicker?

Now look at each stanza and its sound patterns.
- ▶ What consonants are repeated in stanza 3? And stanza 4?
- ▶ Which stanza's lines contain more syllables?

How do you think these factors contribute to the mood and pace of the two stanzas? Write a sentence explaining how the poet uses alliteration to change the speed of the action in these stanzas.

Comprehension

1 Where is the heron in the poem?

 2 What do the words 'gawky' and 'stilted' tell us about the appearance of the heron?

 3 Why is the bird's colour described as 'gun-grey-green'? Why does the poet choose to use the word 'gun' in this phrase? What does it tell us about the heron?

 4 Look at some of the adjectives and adverbs the poet uses in the phrases below to describe the heron's mood and actions:
a) <u>gauntly</u> watchful
b) a <u>brooding</u> hump
c) <u>cold</u>-eye
d) <u>stiff</u> on single column
For each phrase, explain in a sentence what the adjective or adverb tells you about how the heron looks and behaves.

 5 What do you learn about the heron from the line 'scorns the noisy fancy oystercatchers' talk'? How does this show the heron as being apart from the other birds?

6 Look carefully at the way the poet uses punctuation and breaks up the stanzas in the poem.

a) How many full stops are in the poem?

b) Each stanza describes different parts of the heron's life and is connected to the next stanza by a dash (–) showing the passing of time, e.g.

> Stanza 1 – In this stanza the poet describes the physical appearance of the heron. It is seen as motionless and waiting to pounce on his prey. It is a patient and skilled hunter.

Now write a few sentences for stanzas two, three and four, explaining what happens in each of these stanzas.

7 How would you describe the shape of the poem? Think especially about the length of the lines. Is there a phrase in the poem that seems to you to describe the look of the poem on the page? Why do you think the poet has chosen to shape his poem in this way?

Extended response

How does the language of the poem help you to imagine the appearance, mood and behaviour of the heron?

Organize your answer into 3-5 paragraphs and try to include your ideas on some of the following:

▶ words used to describe what the heron looks like
▶ phrases that suggest the heron is apart from the other birds
▶ what the poem tells us about the heron's way of hunting
▶ how the poem's shape helps us imagine the heron
▶ how the poem uses sound patterning, like rhyme and alliteration.

Speaking and listening

Pair/group

Heron is a poem best appreciated read aloud. Prepare a pair or group reading of the poem in which you try to bring out the sound patterns.

Start by preparing a copy of the poem to use as a script. Use different colours to underline or highlight the various uses of rhyme, alliteration and repetition. This will help you to bring them out in your reading.

TEXT B

H ere is another poem in which shape and sound help to convey meaning. It is also written by a Scottish poet, Jackie Kay.

Hairpin Bend

Around the hairpin
bends
   where the drop
down
   gives you vertigo
and
   you cling
to the steering wheel,
   there are
   mountain goats
who
   ring their bells
while
   you get dizzy
      and even
         dizzier,
they are just happy –
long beards
      shaking –
probably
   laughing
      a goat's guffaw
at the tourist's
      silly fear of heights.

Aaaargh. Help.

Jackie Kay

WORD BANK

guffaw a coarse, noisy
   laugh
hairpin bend a sharp
   V-shaped bend in a road
vertigo dizziness
   associated with a fear
   of heights

Comparison

 This is another poem where the layout helps to tell us what the poem is about. How does the layout of the words on the page in *Hairpin Bend* suggest what it is about?

 Why do you think Jackie Kay has chosen to address the reader directly as 'you' in this poem?

Can you find any examples of any types of sound pattern (alliteration and rhyme) in the poem? List them.

 What do you think of the way the poem ends? What has happened? Do you find the ending surprising, scary, funny?

Write a paragraph comparing the layout of the two poems: *Heron* and *Hairpin Bend*. The following questions should help you:
▷ Describe the shape of each poem. How does it help the reader to understand the poem?
▷ How do the two poets use punctuation and different line lengths to help shape their poems?

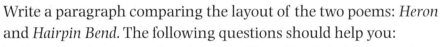

Writing assignments

1 Write a shape poem: a poem with its words arranged in the shape of its subject, just as Jackie Kay makes *Hairpin Bend* look like a steep, winding road on the page.
Some ideas might include a poem about a rollercoaster, a children's playground or a classroom – you could arrange the words like pupils sitting at desks.
Also try to include in your poem some of the sound features you have learnt about in this unit – alliteration and rhyme. (For a reminder of these features, look back at the Language focus on p138.)

2 Find a poem you like that is set out traditionally. Create a new version of the poem where you do not alter any of the words themselves but you change the size and shape of the lettering, the colour and layout, in order to emphasize the words' meaning. Be as imaginative as possible. You can do this by hand, or you might be able to create your text using a compuuter. Below is an example to help you. It is a rearrangement of a famous nineteenth-century poem called *The Kraken* by Alfred, Lord Tennyson, about an imaginary sea monster.

The Kraken

Below the thunders of the upper deep;

Far, far beneath in the ABYSMAL sea,

His ancient, dreamless, uninvaded sleep, Zzzzzzzz

The Kraken sleepeth: faintest sunlights flee

About his shadowy sides: above him swell

Huge sponges of millennial **growth** and height;

And far away into the sickly light,

From many a wondrous grot and secret cell

Unnumber'd and **enormous polypi**

Winnow with giant arms the slumbering *green*.

There hath he lain for ages and will lie

Battening upon **huge seaworms** in his sleep,

Until the latter **fire** shall **heat** the deep;

Then once by men and angels to be seen,

In RO A R Ing he shall rise and on the surface die.

Alfred, Lord Tennyson

Poetry
Imagery – word pictures

Aims

In this unit you will:

▷ learn about two poetic devices: simile and metaphor

▷ study two nature poems which use similes and metaphors

▷ look at the effects of these devices on the reader

▷ write your own poem which uses imagery.

Language focus

Poets use words to try to create vivid and effective images in their readers' minds. Imagery is the name we give to a series of images in a poem or novel. Writers use two main devices to create fresh and imaginative images. These are **simile** and **metaphor**. In both devices, one thing is compared to another.

For example, if I want to say that my brother is really untidy and messy, I may choose to use the following comparisons:

My brother – A pig	His room – A pig-sty

Simile and metaphor differ in the way they structure the comparison.

Simile

Here, one thing is compared to another using the linking words 'like' or 'as' e.g. My brother eats like a pig and his room is as messy as a pig-sty.

Metaphor

Here, one thing is compared to another without using the linking words 'like' or 'as'. It is more direct than a simile – one thing is actually said to be the other e.g. My brother is a pig. His room is a pig-sty.

Images can be visual (i.e. they create a mental picture), or they can appeal to our other senses, such as hearing, taste or smell. They also may rely on **word associations**: feelings which words create in the reader. For example, a heart is often associated with emotions, particularly love, and also romance and courage.

TEXT A

Theodore Roethke was an American poet, born in 1908. He wrote many descriptive poems which often use images of childhood and of nature. His poetry collections include *Open House*, 1941, and *The Waking*, 1953, for which he was awarded a Pulitzer prize. He died in 1963.

The Meadow Mouse

I

In a shoe box stuffed in an old nylon stocking
Sleeps the baby mouse I found in the meadow,
Where he trembled and shook beneath a stick
Till I caught him up by the tail and brought him in,
Cradled in my hand,
A little quaker, the whole body of him trembling,
His absurd whiskers sticking out like a cartoon-mouse,
His feet like small leaves,
Little lizard-feet,
Whitish and spread wide when he tried to struggle away,
Wriggling like a minuscule puppy.

Now he's eaten his three kinds of cheese and drunk from
    his bottle-cap watering-trough –
So much he just lies in one corner,
His tail curled under him, his belly big
As his head, his bat-like ears
Twitching, tilting toward the least sound.

Do I imagine he no longer trembles
When I come close to him?
He seems no longer to tremble.

WORD BANK

by courtesy of as a favour from

forsaken deserted, abandoned, without help or friendship

hapless unfortunate, unlucky

minuscule extremely small

nestling a bird that cannot yet fly

paralytic a person who is paralysed

shrike carnivorous bird which preys on mice

II

But this morning the shoe-box house on the back porch is empty.
Where has he gone, my meadow mouse,
My thumb of a child that nuzzled in my palm? –
To run under the hawk's wing,
Under the eye of the great owl watching from the elm-tree,
To live by courtesy of the shrike, the snake, the tom-cat.

I think of the nestling fallen into the deep grass,
The turtle gasping in the dusty rubble of the highway,
The paralytic stunned in the tub, and the water rising, –
All things innocent, hapless, forsaken.

Theodore Roethke

Language questions

 1 Find five examples of similes from the poem.

 2 For each simile, say what is being compared to what. Try to explain what you think is effective about it. An answer for the first simile in the poem is given as an example:

> 'like a cartoon-mouse' – this simile compares the real mouse to a cartoon mouse. It is an effective simile because it shows us how the mouse's whiskers stick out in a comical way and how it looks a bit like a mouse in a cartoon, drawn in an exaggerated way.

 3 The poem also contains many examples of metaphors. Look at the following phrases from the poem which all use metaphors. These have been underlined.
- ▶ 'little <u>lizard-feet</u>'
- ▶ 'his bottle-cap <u>watering-trough</u>'
- ▶ 'the <u>shoe-box house</u>'
- ▶ 'my <u>thumb of a child</u>'

For each example on the previous page, write one or two sentences explaining how the metaphor works. What is being compared to what? How does the metaphor help us imagine what is being described? What are its effects?
An answer to the first one is given as an example.

> 'little lizard-feet' compares the mouse's feet to a lizard's. It suggests the feet are scaly and rough, like a lizard's. It helps us imagine more exactly the texture and appearance of the feet.

4 The metaphors in question 3 are all nouns, but writers can use verbs as metaphors too. For example, if we say, 'Jane was late for work. She grabbed her coat and flew out of the house'; we do not mean she was literally flying, we use the verb 'flew' as a metaphor. She is running so fast, her speed is compared to flying.

Find an example of a verb used as a metaphor in the poem. Try to explain why it is a metaphor – what is being compared to what?
Hint It compares the poet's hand to something.

Comprehension

1 Where is the mouse at the beginning of the poem?

2 Where did the narrator find the mouse and how did he/she catch it?

3 Write down the words and phrases the narrator uses to describe the mouse in the first stanza. Looking at these words and phrases, how do you think the narrator sees the mouse?

4 The narrator feels he/she cares very much for the mouse. What words and phrases from the first two stanzas can you find which suggest this?

5 a) What words or phrases in stanza 1 show that the mouse is scared?
b) Is it still scared at the end of stanza 2? Back up your opinion with a quotation from this stanza.

6 What has happened at the beginning of Part II of the poem?

7 Think about the line 'Where has he gone, my meadow mouse'. What does the use of the possessive 'my' here suggest about how the narrator feels towards the mouse?

8 What dangers does the narrator imagine might threaten the mouse now it is living in the wild?

9 In the final stanza, to what does the narrator compare the meadow mouse's plight? In what way does he/she see all these things as similar?

Extended response

Look at these two statements about 'The Meadow Mouse'.

A We are meant to sympathize with the narrator, who is trying to save the mouse from the hazards of the wild.

B We are not meant to sympathize with the narrator, who has taken the mouse out of the wild where it belongs.

Which of these statements do you think best sums up the message of the poem?

To start with, collect information in a grid like this. Some pieces of information can be interpreted in both ways – it's up to you to decide which side of the grid to put them in. For instance:

A Sympathetic narrator saving mouse	B Unsympathetic narrator keeping mouse captive
'Three kinds of cheese' – narrator makes sure mouse has food	'Three kinds of cheese' – a meadow mouse wouldn't normally eat cheese – only mice in cartoons do this. Narrator is well-meaning but not really helping the mouse.

Then write up your answer, backing it up with the evidence you have found.

Speaking and listening

Class

As a class, discuss this question: Should animals be kept by people, for their own protection?
Different aspects you can consider:

keeping pets

▶ could these animals live in the wild?
▶ are they the same as wild breeds of animal?
▶ do humans benefit from keeping pets?
▶ do pets like living with humans?

keeping animals in zoos

▶ is captivity harmful to the animals?
▶ are animals happy in zoos?
▶ would the animals survive in the wild?
▶ should animals which are hunted be protected?
▶ can all animals breed successfully in the wild?
▶ are there any other effective ways to save animals whose habitats are being destroyed?

Before the discussion, write down a point to raise, and try to find some evidence to back up your view.
Everyone should contribute to the discussion, with the teacher acting as chair if necessary. At the end of the discussion, hold a vote to see what the overall class view is.

TEXT B

Norman MacCaig was born in 1910, the son of an Edinburgh chemist and a Gaelic-speaking mother from the Hebridean island of Scalpay. He read Classics at Edinburgh University and was a primary school teacher and headmaster from 1934 to 67, except for the war years when he was a conscientious objector – someone whose beliefs make them refuse to fight. He lectured in English, poetry and creative writing at various Scottish universities until 1977. He is regarded as one of the most influential Scottish poets of the 20th Century. He died in 1996.

Toad

Stop looking like a purse. How could a purse
squeeze under the rickety door and sit,
full of satisfaction, in a man's house?

You clamber towards me on your four corners –
right hand, left foot, left hand, right foot.

I love you for being a toad,
for crawling like a Japanese wrestler,
and for not being frightened.

I put you in my purse hand, not shutting it,
and set you down outside directly under
every star.

A jewel in your head? Toad,
you've put one in mine,
a tiny radiance in a dark place.

Norman MacCaig

WORD BANK

clamber climb with difficulty, using hands and feet
jewel in your head myth has it that the toad grows a precious jewel in its head which acts as an antidote to poison
radiance dazzling brightness
rickety poorly constructed, likely to collapse

Comparison

1. For each of the following images from *Toad*, complete the chart below, saying whether the image is a simile or a metaphor.

Image	Simile or metaphor?
'like a purse'	
'your four corners'	
'like a Japanese wrestler'	
'my purse hand'	

2. Why do you think the poet compares the toad to a purse?

3. What impressions do you get of the appearance and movements of the toad from the lines:

> 'You clamber towards me on your four corners –
> right hand, left foot, left hand, right foot,'
> *and*
> 'crawling like a Japanese wrestler'?

4. The poet says that he 'loves' the toad. What three reasons does he give for this?

5. In the last stanza of the poem, the poet refers to the myth of the toad growing a jewel in its head, a rare antidote to poison. What do you think the poet means when he says

> 'Toad,
> you've put one in mine,
> a tiny radiance in a dark place'?

6. Both poems are about relationships with animals. Write a few sentences describing the two narrators' feelings for the animals in the poems. Think about:
   ▶ how the narrators meet the animals
   ▶ how the narrators react to their presence (what they do)

▶ what the narrators say about their feelings for the animals
▶ the narrators 'attitudes to the animals' natural environment
▶ how the narrators feel at the end of the poems.

Writing assignments

1 You are going to write your own animal poem. Firstly, you need to choose an animal to describe. Then brainstorm what you already know about this animal – its appearance, the way it moves, the sounds it makes, its environment, etc.

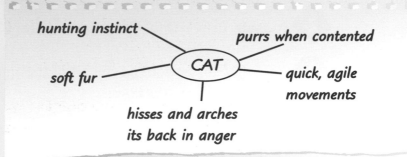

hunting instinct
purrs when contented
soft fur
CAT
quick, agile movements
hisses and arches its back in anger

You are now going to use these ideas to write a first draft of your poem. You may just describe the animal or you may want the poem to tell a short story like *The Meadow Mouse*.

Try to make the way you use language as precise and as imaginative as you can. Also, try to use at least three similes and metaphors in your poem. (You can look back at the Language focus on p146 to remind yourself how similes and metaphors 'work'.)

To help you think of lively and unusual comparisons, you could play 'The Furniture Game'. In this, you answer imaginary questions to help you make connections.

Start by making a list of questions like:

▶ If this animal were a piece of furniture, what would it be?
▶ If it were a food, what would it be?
▶ If it were an item of clothing, what would it be?
▶ If it were a month of the year, what would it be?

Then answer your questions. Your answers may suggest some interesting similes or metaphors.

When you are happy with your redrafted poem, you may want to create an illustrated version.

2 Write a short information text (150-200 words) about an animal to appear as a page for a CD-Rom encyclopaedia. You could write about the same animal as in the poem or you may choose a different animal.

First you will need to research your chosen animal. Use reference books and CD-Roms to find out as much as you can, as you are going to have to present facts here.
Remember:
- the purpose of your text is to inform your reader
- try to write 150-200 words
- write in a clear, informative style.

Try to lay out your text in a clear and eye-catching way: use titles, sub-titles, bold type, colour, bullet points and other devices to present the information.

Glossary

Accent   The way somebody pronounces words, which usually depends on where they were brought up or the people they have spent most time with.

Active verb   A verb which describes something that is happening, rather than saying how something is, e.g. *the leaves **turn** yellow, the cat **purred** on the windowsill*. (See **Stative verb** to compare the two.)

Adjective   A word that describes a noun and adds more information to it, e.g. *a **blue** balloon; a **lonely** boy; a **sad** day*.

Adverb   A word that describes a verb and adds more information to it, e.g. *she left **suddenly**; he spoke **loudly***.

Alliteration   The effect you get when several words next to or near each other begin with the same sound, e.g. ***big, bold** and **brassy***.

Apostrophe   The punctuation mark (') which can be used in two ways:
   1 to show that a letter or group of letters has been missed out, e.g. *I'm not going; We'll be there*.
   2 to show that someone owns or has something, e.g. *Peter's mum; Helen's bag*.

Audience   The people a piece of writing is aimed at; or the people who watch a film, play or television programme.

Blank verse   A kind of verse that does not rhyme. Shakespeare wrote his plays in blank verse.

Character   A person in a story, play, or poem.

Chorus   A group of actors who speak alone or together to create a range of effects in a play.

Clause   A part of a sentence which is actually made up of a simple sentence. Some sentences have a **main clause** and a **subordinate clause**, e.g. *I was reading a book* (main clause) *when the telephone rang* (subordinate clause). The **main clause** can stand on its own. The **subordinate clause** adds extra meaning to the sentence but does not make sense on its own.

Comparison   A way of describing one thing by saying it is like another, e.g. *The fence was broken into stumps **like a tramp's teeth***.

Complex sentence   A sentence which contains more than one idea and is made up of a main clause and a subordinate clause. [See page 95 for an explanation of how complex sentences are made up.] e.g. *As soon as I saw the lions, I ran away. Although I ran fast, they soon caught up with me*.

Compound sentence   A sentence which contains more than one idea, where the clauses are joined by *and, but*, or *or*, e.g. *I saw the lions **and** I ran away. I ran fast, **but** they ran faster. I had to escape **or** they would eat me*.

Contraction   Words which have been joined together, with some of the letters missed out, e.g. ***we're*** (not *we are*); ***I'll*** (not *I will*); *they **won't*** (not *they will not*).

Dialect   A variation of a language, which has its own grammatical rules and its own words and expressions. A dialect is usually spoken by people who come from a particular area or cultural background.

Dialogue   The words spoken by the characters in a play or story.

Discourse markers Words and phrases which link a text together and help the reader follow how the text is developing, e.g. *then, later, therefore, whilst*.

Emotive vocabulary Words which cause an emotional response in the reader, e.g. *horror, shocked, disaster*.

End rhyme A rhyme where the last word of a line of poetry rhymes with the last word of another line.

Exclamation mark The punctuation mark (!) used at the end of a sentence. It can show, for example, that a command has been given or that something is said urgently or in surprise, e.g. *'Come here!'*; *'I can't!'*; *It was Joe!*

Fact Something that is true, and not just an opinion, e.g. *The Earth moves around the Sun.*

First person See **Narrative viewpoint** and **Person of the verb**.

Formal language Language which does not contain slang, and where all or most of the sentences are complete and 'grammatically correct' (i.e. in Standard English).

Formal letter A letter that follows all the rules of grammar and presentation. [To see how a formal letter is laid out, see page 19.]

Formal style A style that follows all the rules of grammar. [See pages 96-97 for more details on the differences between formal and informal style.]

Full rhyme A rhyme where two words rhyme completely, e.g. *cry / dry; full / pull*.

Full stop The punctuation mark (.) used at the end of most sentences.

Future tense The form of a verb which shows that what it describes has not yet happened, or is about to happen, e.g. *I **will feed** the cat soon. In 2050, people **will go** on holiday to the moon.*

Half rhyme A rhyme where the words have similar sounds but do not rhyme completely, e.g. *town / stone*.

Imperative The command form of a verb, used for giving orders or instructions, e.g. ***Get off*** *the roof!*; ***Take*** *a clean piece of paper*; *Please **help** me*.

Infinitive The 'original state' of a verb, when it does not tell you about who is doing it or when, e.g. *to fly, to see, to be*.

Informal language Language that breaks the rules of grammar by using slang, changing sentence structure and sometimes appearing more like spoken than written language.

Informal letter A letter written in a style which is more like speech than formal writing. It may not follow all the rules of grammar and presentation. [To see how an informal letter is usually laid out, see page 19.]

Informal style A style which is more like speech than formal writing. It may not follow all the rules of grammar. [See pages 96-97 for more details on the differences between formal and informal style.]

Internal rhyme A rhyme where a word in the middle of a line rhymes with the one at the end.

Irregular verb A verb which does not follow the pattern of regular verbs. *To be, to have* and *to go* are very common irregular verbs. With some, you can only see they are irregular when you form their past tense, which does not end in **ed** or **d**, e.g. *to ride: I rode; to feel: I felt; to sit: I sat*.

Main clause See **Clause**.

Metaphor A way of comparing one thing with another, but without using *like* or *as*: one thing is actually said to be the other, e.g. *My room is a shoe-box*.

Narrative voice/viewpoint Whether a piece of writing is written in the first person (e.g. *I walked up the lane*: as if one of the characters is telling the story) or the third person (e.g. *He walked up the lane*: as if another person is telling the reader what the characters did, said, and felt). The third person allows the writer to show the point of view of more than one character.

Narrator The person who tells a story. This can be a person who tells the story from the outside, or someone who is involved in the story. See also **Narrative viewpoint**.

Noun The word in a sentence which labels a person, place, thing, idea, or feeling, e.g. ***Jenny** felt a **wave** of **tiredness** as she walked down the **street***.

Opinion Something that is not a fact, but someone's point of view, e.g. *The garden is charming*.

Paragraph A block of sentences linked by one overall idea or topic, e.g. the first paragraph under Text A on page 51 contains three sentences, all about the childhood of Charles Dickens.

Participle Part of a verb that can be used to make up compound verb forms, e.g. *she is **going**, he has **gone***. It can also be used as an adjective, e.g. ***cooking** utensils, **cooked** meat*.

Past tense The form of a verb which shows that the action it describes is complete or happened in the past, e.g. *I **went** swimming today. Queen Elizabeth the First **had** red hair*.

Person of the verb The part of the verb according to who is doing it. The first person singular ('I') or plural ('we') is the most personal to use. The second person singular and plural ('you') is used to address the reader. The third person singular ('he'/'she'/'it') or plural ('they') is the least personal, and is used a lot in stories.

Personification Writing about an object or an idea as if it were a person, e.g. *The computer **is in a bad mood** today*.

Phrase A group of words which makes sense inside a clause or sentence, but cannot stand on its own, e.g. *running around; on a bike*.

Present tense The form of a verb which shows that the action it describes is happening now, happens regularly, or usually happens, e.g. *I **am doing** my homework* (now), *I **do** my homework in the sitting room* (regularly or usually).

Presentational devices Ways of laying out a text, also known as 'design features', such as titles, captions, bullet points, and bold lettering. [See page 6 for a list of presentational devices used in newspaper articles.]

Pronoun A word that can replace a noun, to avoid repetition, e.g. *I, it, he, she, they, we*.

Pun A sort of joke made by using a word or phrase that can have more than one meaning, or that sounds very like a phrase with a different meaning, e.g. *Ornamental stones now at rock bottom prices*: *rock* as in 'stones' and *rock bottom* meaning 'cheap'.

Punctuation The marks we use in writing to make it easier to read and understand. [See also **Apostrophe**, **Exclamation mark**, **Full stop**.]

Purpose The reason a writer has for writing a text; e.g. to give information, to persuade somebody, or to entertain.

Refrain A line which is repeated at intervals in a song, ballad, or poem.

Regular verb A verb which follows a regular pattern, where the he/she/it form in the present tense ends with **s** or **es**, and the past tense ends with **d** or **ed**, e.g. *to cook*: *it cooks, we cooked*; *to try*: *she tries, I tried*; *to grumble*: *he grumbles, they grumbled*.

Rhetorical question A question which is asked for effect, rather than to get information, e.g. *What's the point?*

Rhyme Words rhyme when their endings have the same sounds, e.g. *bend / send*.

Rhyme scheme The pattern of rhymes inside a poem.

Rhyming couplet A rhyme scheme where one line of poetry rhymes with the line that comes next after it, e.g.
Mary had a little lamb
She tried to feed it peas and ham.

Rhythm The 'beat' of a poem. The rhythm might be fast, smooth, or irregular, for example. A limerick has a very noticeable rhythm.

Simile A way of comparing one thing with another, using the words *like* or *as*, e.g. *My house is **like** a shed. My room is **as** small **as** a shoe-box.*

Simple sentence A sentence which is made of only one clause and which has only one main point, e.g. *Alan joined the football team.* The meaning of a simple sentence is very clear.

Slang A very informal kind of language, often belonging to a particular group of people, e.g. army slang, Australian slang.

Stage directions The instructions telling an actor how to speak or move on the stage, and what emotions to show.

Stanza A group of lines in a poem (also called a verse). Each stanza is separated from the next by a space.

Stative verb A verb that describes how something is, rather than saying what it is doing, e.g. *the leaves **are** yellow, the cat **was** on the windowsill.* [See **Active verb** to compare the two.]

Subordinate clause See **Clause**.

Syllable Part of a word, taking up one beat, e.g. *sit* has one syllable, *sitting* has two, and *syllable* has three.

Tabloid newspaper A newspaper with a small format, aimed at general readers. Tabloid papers have large headlines and a lot of pictures. They often focus on stories about famous people, crime, and scandals.

Tense The feature of a verb's form that shows when the action it describes is happening.

Third person See **Narrative viewpoint**, and **Person of the verb**.

Tone The atmosphere of a piece of writing: whether it is serious or comic, for example.

Verb The word in a sentence which says what people or things are doing, e.g. *He **danced** and **sang***; or what they are being, e.g. *The room **was** dark.*

Acknowledgements

We are grateful for permission to reprint the following copyright material.

Steve Barlow and Steve Skidmore: extract from *A Tale of Two Cities* (OUP, 1996) adapted from the novel by Charles Dickens, reprinted by permission of Oxford University Press; **Elizabeth Bishop**: 'The Burglar of Babylon' from *The Complete Poems* (1983) copyright 1940, 1944, 1955, 1962, 1964, 1969 and renewed 1972, reprinted by permission of Farrar, Straus & Giroux Inc.; **James Blish**: extract from 'Common Time' from *Galactic Cluster* (Faber), reprinted by permission of Laurence Pollinger Ltd and the Estate of James Blish; **David Calcutt**: extract from *The Labyrinth* (OUP, 2000), reprinted by permission of Oxford University Press; adaptation of Shakespeare's *Henry V*, copyright © David Calcutt 2000, first published here by permission of the author; **Richard Curtis and Ben Elton**: extract from 'Blackadder Goes Forth' from *Blackadder: The Whole Damn Dynasty* (Michael Joseph, 1998), copyright © Richard Curtis and Ben Elton 1987, reprinted by permission of Penguin Books Ltd.; **Jackie Kay**: 'Hairpin Bend' from *Two's Company* (Blackie, 1992), copyright © Jackie Kay 1992, reprinted by permission of Penguin Books Ltd.; **Laurie Lee**: extract from *Cider with Rosie* (Penguin, 1998), reprinted by permission of the Peters Fraser & Dunlop Group Ltd.; **Andy Lines**: 'He's huge, he's powerful, he's fast and he's mean: two million flee from Hurricane Floyd', *The Mirror*, 15.9.99, reprinted by permission of Mirror Syndication International; **Norman MacCaig**: 'Toad' from *Collected Poems* (The Hogarth Press, 1985), reprinted by permission of the Random House Group Ltd.; **Edwin Morgan**: 'Heron' from *Uncollected Poems 1949-1982* (1990), reprinted by permission of the publishers, Carcanet Press Ltd.; **Michael Morpurgo**: extract from *The Wreck of the Zanzibar* (Heinemann Young Books & Mammoth, imprints of Egmont Children's Books Ltd), text copyright © Michael Morpurgo 1995; illustration by Christian Birmingham, illustrations copyright © Christian Birmingham 1995; reprinted by permission of Egmont Children's Books Ltd.; **Oxford School Shakespeare**, extract from *Henry V* edited by Roma Gill, reprinted by permission of Oxford University Press; **Nick Page**: 'French Fried Crisp'n' Die' from Nick Page: *The Bard – The Tabloid Shakespeare* (1999), reprinted by permission of HarperCollins Publishers Ltd.; **Samuel Pepys**: extract from *The Diary of Samuel Pepys* edited by Robert Latham and William Matthews (HarperCollins, 1983), copyright © The Masters, Fellows, and Scholars of Magdalene College, Cambridge, Robert Latham and William Matthews 1983, reprinted by permission of PFD on behalf of the Masters, Fellows, and Scholars of Magdalene College Cambridge, the Estate of Robert Latham and the Estate of Lois Emery Matthews; **Rosemary Rhodes**: Letter to Megan, December 1999, reprinted by permission of Rosemary Rhodes; **Theodore Roethke**: 'The Meadow Mouse' from *Collected Poems of Theodore Roethke* (1968), reprinted by permission of the publishers, Faber & Faber Ltd.; **Arundhati Roy**: extract from *The God of Small Things* (Flamingo, 1997), reprinted by permission of HarperCollins Publishers Ltd.; RSPCA: campaign letter reprinted by permission of the **RSPCA** and Target Direct Marketing.

Although every effort has been made to trace and contact copyright holders before publication this has not been possible in some cases. If notified the publisher will be pleased to rectify any errors or omissions at the earliest opportunity.

We would like to thank the following for permission to include photographs:

p8 (top & bottom) Popperfoto; p13 *Portrait of Samuel Pepys*, copy after J. Riley by Johann Baptiste Closterman, Philip Mould Historical Portraits London, UK/Bridgeman Art Library; *Great Fire of London*, Dutch School, London Museum/Art Archive; pp21/22 RSPCA; p26 Express Newspapers; p29 Joe McDonald/CORBIS; p36 Rex Features; p44 (top) Peters Fraser & Dunlop; p44 (bottom) Rex Features; p46 BBC Picture Archives; p47 BBC Picture Archives; p51 *Charles Dickens* by William Powell Frith, Victoria & Albert Museum, UK/ Bridgeman Art Library; p52 Steve Barlow (top), Steve Skidmore (bottom); p55 *Duc de Boufflers and enraged crowds*, Maurice Le Loir, AKG London; p60 David Calcutt; p70 Mary Evans Picture Library; p71/72 Kobal Collection; p91 Science Photo Library; p97 Egmont Children's Books; p106 Ronald Grant Archive; p111 Rex Features, photo Julian Makey; p116 (top) *Robert Hooke*, AKG London; p116 (bottom) Bruce Coleman Collection, photo Alan Stillwell; p125 *Sailing Ship in Rough Seas*, by Philip J. Ouless, Christie's Images; p130 Camera Press, photo B. Silberstein; p138 (left) Camera Press, photo Jessie Ann Matthew; p138 (right) Clive Druett; Papilio/CORBIS; p146 Robert Harding Picture Library; p151 Bruce Coleman Collection, photo Rod Williams.

The illustrations are by: Michael Frith p37; Roger Gorringe p117; Lee Sullivan p62.

Cover image: Digital Vision